Abortion

Other Books of Related Interest:

Opposing Viewpoints Series

Universal Health Care

At Issue Series

Do Abstinence Programs Work?

Current Controversies Series

Teen Pregancy and Parenting

"Congress shall make no law . . . abridging the freedom of speech, or of the press."

First Amendment to the U.S. Constitution

The basic foundation of our democracy is the First Amendment guarantee of freedom of expression. The Opposing Viewpoints Series is dedicated to the concept of this basic freedom and the idea that it is more important to practice it than to enshrine it.

OPPOSING VIEWPOINTS® SERIES

| Abortion

David Haugen, Susan Musser, and Kacy Lovelace,
book editors

GREENHAVEN PRESS
A part of Gale, Cengage Learning

GALE
CENGAGE Learning™

Detroit • New York • San Francisco • New Haven, Conn • Waterville, Maine • London

Christine Nasso, *Publisher*
Elizabeth Des Chenes, *Managing Editor*

© 2010 Greenhaven Press, a part of Gale, Cengage Learning.

Gale and Greenhaven Press are registered trademarks used herein under license.

For more information, contact:
Greenhaven Press
27500 Drake Rd.
Farmington Hills, MI 48331-3535
Or you can visit our Internet site at gale.cengage.com

For product information and technology assistance, contact us at

Gale Customer Support, 1-800-877-4253
For permission to use material from this text or product, submit all requests online at
www.cengage.com/permissions

Further permissions questions can be emailed to permissionrequest@cengage.com

Articles in Greenhaven Press anthologies are often edited for length to meet page requirements. In addition, original titles of these works are changed to clearly present the main thesis and to explicitly indicate the author's opinion. Every effort is made to ensure that Greenhaven Press accurately reflects the original intent of the authors. Every effort has been made to trace the owners of copyrighted material.

Cover Image copyright © Zothen/Dreamstime.com.

LIBRARY OF CONGRESS CATALOGING-IN-PUBLICATION DATA

Abortion / David Haugen, Susan Musser, and Kacy Lovelace, book editors.
   p. cm. -- (Opposing viewpoints)
   Includes bibliographical references and index.
   ISBN 978-0-7377-4747-8 (hardcover) -- ISBN 978-0-7377-4748-5 (pbk.)
   1. Abortion--Juvenile literature. I. Haugen, David M., 1969- II. Musser, Susan. III. Lovelace, Kacy.
   HQ767.A152 2010
   362.19'888--dc22

                                                2009041649

Printed in the United States of America
1 2 3 4 5 6 7 14 13 12 11 10

Contents

Why Consider Opposing Viewpoints?

> *"The only way in which a human being can make some approach to knowing the whole of a subject is by hearing what can be said about it by persons of every variety of opinion and studying all modes in which it can be looked at by every character of mind. No wise man ever acquired his wisdom in any mode but this."*
>
> John Stuart Mill

In our media-intensive culture it is not difficult to find differing opinions. Thousands of newspapers and magazines and dozens of radio and television talk shows resound with differing points of view. The difficulty lies in deciding which opinion to agree with and which "experts" seem the most credible. The more inundated we become with differing opinions and claims, the more essential it is to hone critical reading and thinking skills to evaluate these ideas. Opposing Viewpoints books address this problem directly by presenting stimulating debates that can be used to enhance and teach these skills. The varied opinions contained in each book examine many different aspects of a single issue. While examining these conveniently edited opposing views, readers can develop critical thinking skills such as the ability to compare and contrast authors' credibility, facts, argumentation styles, use of persuasive techniques, and other stylistic tools. In short, the Opposing Viewpoints Series is an ideal way to attain the higher-level thinking and reading skills so essential in a culture of diverse and contradictory opinions.

In addition to providing a tool for critical thinking, Opposing Viewpoints books challenge readers to question their own strongly held opinions and assumptions. Most people form their opinions on the basis of upbringing, peer pressure, and personal, cultural, or professional bias. By reading carefully balanced opposing views, readers must directly confront new ideas as well as the opinions of those with whom they disagree. This is not to simplistically argue that everyone who reads opposing views will—or should—change his or her opinion. Instead, the series enhances readers' understanding of their own views by encouraging confrontation with opposing ideas. Careful examination of others' views can lead to the readers' understanding of the logical inconsistencies in their own opinions, perspective on why they hold an opinion, and the consideration of the possibility that their opinion requires further evaluation.

Evaluating Other Opinions

To ensure that this type of examination occurs, Opposing Viewpoints books present all types of opinions. Prominent spokespeople on different sides of each issue as well as well-known professionals from many disciplines challenge the reader. An additional goal of the series is to provide a forum for other, less known, or even unpopular viewpoints. The opinion of an ordinary person who has had to make the decision to cut off life support from a terminally ill relative, for example, may be just as valuable and provide just as much insight as a medical ethicist's professional opinion. The editors have two additional purposes in including these less known views. One, the editors encourage readers to respect others' opinions—even when not enhanced by professional credibility. It is only by reading or listening to and objectively evaluating others' ideas that one can determine whether they are worthy of consideration. Two, the inclusion of such viewpoints encourages the important critical thinking skill of objectively evaluating an author's credentials and bias. This evaluation will illuminate an author's reasons for taking a particular stance on an issue and will aid in readers' evaluation of the author's ideas.

It is our hope that these books will give readers a deeper understanding of the issues debated and an appreciation of the complexity of even seemingly simple issues when good and honest people disagree. This awareness is particularly important in a democratic society such as ours in which people enter into public debate to determine the common good. Those with whom one disagrees should not be regarded as enemies but rather as people whose views deserve careful examination and may shed light on one's own.

Thomas Jefferson once said that "difference of opinion leads to inquiry, and inquiry to truth." Jefferson, a broadly educated man, argued that "if a nation expects to be ignorant and free . . . it expects what never was and never will be." As individuals and as a nation, it is imperative that we consider the opinions of others and examine them with skill and discernment. The Opposing Viewpoints Series is intended to help readers achieve this goal.

David L. Bender and Bruno Leone,
Founders

Introduction

> "This right of privacy, whether it be founded in the Fourteenth Amendment's concept of personal liberty and restrictions upon state action, as we feel it is ... is broad enough to encompass a woman's decision whether to terminate her pregnancy. The detriment that the State would impose upon the pregnant woman by denying this choice altogether is apparent. Specific and direct harm medically diagnosable even in early pregnancy may be involved. Maternity, or additional offspring, may force upon the woman a distressful life and future. Psychological harm may be imminent. Mental and physical health may be taxed by child care. There is also the distress, for all concerned, associated with the unwanted child, and there is the problem of bringing a child into a family already unable, psychologically and otherwise, to care for it."
>
> *Justice Harold Blackmun,*
> *Opinion of the Court,*
> Roe v. Wade *(410 U.S. 113)*

An abortion is any procedure that removes a fetus from a woman's womb. Abortion ends a pregnancy and terminates a fetus's life.

In 1973, 615,831 legal abortions were performed in the United States. That year is significant because before 1973, abortion—unless necessary to save a woman's life—was considered a criminal act in most states. Doctors who performed abortions could be arrested, lose their medical licenses, and end up in prison. Some doctors still offered the procedure, but records indicating how many abortions took place—records that could be used as evidence against the doctors—were scarce or nonexistent.

All that changed on January 22, 1973, when the Supreme Court issued its decision in the *Roe v. Wade* case. The majority of the justices decided that denying an abortion to a woman violated her right to privacy under the Fourteenth Amendment of the U.S. Constitution. Their reasoning was that during the early stage of her pregnancy, a woman has the right to decide whether she will or will not bear the child. A state could not interfere with that right by passing laws that criminalized abortion. The decision was not unanimous, though, as two of the seven justices dissented.

The number of legal abortions performed in the United States rose throughout the 1970s and 1980s. According to the Centers for Disease Control and Prevention (CDC), the highest number of abortions—1,429,577—occurred in 1990. After that peak, a decline began. By 1995 the number had dropped to under 1 million and has remained constant since. In 2005—the last year with published statistics from the CDC—820,151 abortions were performed in the United States. Within these figures, not all socioeconomic groups are equally represented. For thirty-five years the majority of women who procured an abortion have been unmarried (up to 83 percent in recent years) and over a third of the women were African American. The Guttmacher Institute, which gathers statistical data on abortions, reports that the abortion rate among poor women is four times the rate among wealthy women.

The debate over abortion has divided people into two camps: pro-life and pro-choice. Pro-life groups are against abortion and would like to see *Roe v. Wade* overturned, making abortion illegal once again. Their reasons are often religious, and most believe that human life begins at conception. These advocates contend that the unborn deserve the same respect and protections that are granted to all others. As President George W. Bush stated, "The promises of our Declaration of Independence are not just for the strong, the independent, or the healthy. They are for everyone—including unborn children."

Pro-choice groups defend a woman's right to choose when and how many children she will have. Pro-choice groups do not like the label pro-abortion. Some pro-choice people wish to reduce the number of abortions, but they believe that abortion must be kept available as an option for women who do not wish to carry a pregnancy to term. And pro-choice advocates believe that no matter how difficult the choice, women are rational, moral beings who must be allowed to determine what best suits their needs. As the Reverend Carlton W. Veazey, president of the Religious Coalition for Reproductive Choice (RCRC), has stated, "Men and women are moral agents and equipped to make decisions about even the most difficult and complex matters." Most pro-choice defenders insist that this freedom to choose is especially important to those women in the lower socioeconomic scale, or those who may find it difficult to raise children in single-parent homes or care for them in impoverished circumstances.

Polls have shown that over the decades since *Roe v. Wade*, American sentiments about abortion have changed significantly. The Gallup Poll began asking people in 1976 whether abortions should be legal or illegal in all circumstances or legal only under certain circumstances. From 1976 through 2008, between 48 percent and 55 percent of the population picked "legal only under certain circumstances." Only 20 percent in 1976 felt that abortion should always be legal. That figure rose to 34 percent in the early 1990s, then declined again over the next few years. By 2008, only 23 percent favored unrestricted abortion rights.

Those who felt abortion should always be "illegal in all circumstances" went from 20 percent in 1976 down to 12 percent in 1990, then back up to 22 percent in 2008. This suggests that people with the most extreme views, either for or against legal abortion, are close in number—both in 1976 and today. As *Chicago Tribune* columnist Eric Zorn put it, "Over 34 years, the staunch opponents haven't budged and the middle remains mushy."

In follow-up questions to its abortion polls, Gallup found that since 1995, the number of people who consider themselves pro-choice and pro-life has continually wavered. In 1995, 56 percent answered that they were pro-choice. By 2008, that number dropped to 50 percent. In 2009—one year later—the number identifying as pro-choice dropped to 42 percent, while those claiming to be pro-life rose from 44 percent in 2008 to 51 percent in 2009.

While some argue that these variations indicate that many Americans have changed their minds on the abortion issue, others believe that the labels "pro-choice" and "pro-life" oversimplify the issue. "Most people are neither pro-choice nor pro-life, but both; we cherish life, we value choice, and we trade them off with great reluctance," writes Nancy Gibbs of *Newsweek*. She argues that changing political administrations may play a role in the poll variations. "When the right was in charge, people feared the return of coat hangers [a symbol of illegal, dangerous abortions]. Now that the left leads, they fear abortion on demand." She theorizes that the reason public opinion shifts is to maintain a balance: "People apply the brakes to whichever side has the momentum. The stakes are too high, the pain too private, whatever decision a woman makes, to see the issue treated as an ideological toy or a fundraising tool."

The chapters in *Opposing Viewpoints: Abortion* discuss the issues that have been argued since the *Roe v. Wade* decision made it legal for a woman to chose to have an abortion. Gallup and other polls may show some wavering sentiments, but the arguments for and against abortion have remained consistent. These concepts are explored in chapters that ask "Is Abortion Immoral?" "Should Abortion Rights Be Restricted?" "How Does Abortion Impact Society?" and "Is Abortion Safe?"

In *Roe v. Wade,* the Supreme Court decided abortion's legal status based on an implied right to privacy in the Fourteenth Amendment. Ordinary citizens, however, develop their views on abortion based on personal feelings about religion, ethics, freedom, responsibility, family, quality of life, and a host of other issues. As this anthology illustrates, arguments over abortion are often heated and emotional. After all, this topic deals with issues of grief, regret, and death. And the Supreme Court's decision could be undone if the justices—who are appointed by both liberal and conservative presidents— decide that the earlier court misinterpreted the Constitution. Both pro-choice and pro-life supporters recognize this fact, which is why the issue remains as prominent and contested now as it was more than three decades ago.

CHAPTER 1

Is Abortion Immoral?

Chapter Preface

More than 35 years after *Roe v. Wade* made it legal for a woman to obtain an abortion in the United States, the procedure remains a hotly debated moral, religious, political, and social issue. In a May 2009 poll by the Pew Research Center for the People & the Press, more than six in ten Americans (62 percent) said future Supreme Court decisions on abortion are "very important" to them personally. A majority of Americans also said that abortion should have more restrictions than currently exist. In the same month, a Gallup Poll found that 51 percent of Americans called themselves "pro-life" while 42 percent identified themselves as "pro-choice." This marked the first time (since 1995 when Gallup first posed the question) that a majority of U.S. adults referred to themselves as pro-life.

Without question, abortion is a flashpoint issue rooted in morality and emotion. Religious belief is a chief divide in the debate. In the United States, predominantly Christian ethics inform the antiabortionist view that human life is sacred and should be respected from the moment of conception. In a Pew study, evangelical Christians, for example, report strong beliefs in curbing abortion: 86 percent favor parental consent laws, 79 percent say it would be good to reduce the number of abortions, and 87 percent agree that abortion is sometimes or nearly always morally wrong.

Although some religious individuals promote pro-choice viewpoints, people on this side of the debate typically believe that religious doctrine should not dictate political or health issues. Pro-choice groups argue that abortion must remain a legal option so that women are not forced to surrender rights over their own bodies. They believe that each woman has the legal right to make a choice regarding the continuation or termination of her pregnancy, and many contend that this position is a moral choice as well. Nancy Keenan, president of NARAL Pro-Choice America, says, "Being pro-choice is a moral position. It is time for us to reclaim that ground. We can no longer fight this fight without talking about our faith, our values and our morality."

While both ethical positions remain opposed, most Americans agree that abortion is a negative experience for individuals and society. Kristin Williams, spokeswoman for the Washington, D.C.-based group Faith in Public Life, told a reporter for the New Mexico *Independent*, "What most people do agree on is finding ways to work together to reduce the number of abortions." While many pro-choice advocates may accept that goal, however, they are determined that such aims do not interfere with giving women the option to abort an unwanted pregnancy. The authors in the following chapter examine the moral arguments that surround the abortion debate. Some contend that the issue is black and white, while others suggest that absolutes cloud the issue and stifle meaningful progress toward reducing the occurrence of abortion.

> *"Just as it would be wrong to arbitrarily kill someone like you or me . . . it is equally wrong to kill fetuses, because they also have valuable futures."*

Abortion Is Immoral

Jeff Jones

In the following viewpoint, Jeff Jones maintains that abortion is morally unjustifiable because fetuses, like fully formed human beings, have futures of value. Jones's argument follows one set forth by philosophy professor Don Marquis in 1989. Jones and Marquis believe that abortion should be judged just as any other act of killing is judged. The author contends that taking the life of a human being is wrong because it robs the individual of his or her future; likewise, abortion is wrong because it denies the fetus a future. Jones is the director of ministry outreach at Abort73, the subdivision of the Christian nonprofit education corporation Loxafamosity Ministries, which seeks to spread the idea that abortion is one of the greatest injustices of modern times.

As you read, consider the following questions:

1. What does the author claim both pro-lifers and pro-choicers seek to utilize in their attempts to prove that their particular stance is correct?

Jeff Jones, "A Future Lost," Abort73.com, December 9, 2008. Reproduced by permission.

2. According to philosophy professor Don Marquis, why is killing wrong?

3. In Jeff Jones's view, how are fetuses and humans alike, and what implications does this have for abortion?

Both pro-lifers and pro-choicers make claims about their positions that they take to be quite obvious and sufficient for establishing abortion as either an immoral or a moral practice. On the one side, pro-lifers claim that human life begins at conception. Since this can be established scientifically by looking at the number of chromosomes present in a fertilized egg, it is enough for the pro-lifer to conclude that abortion (at any stage of pregnancy) is morally akin to murder. On the other side, pro-choicers claim that fetuses are quite obviously *not* persons. Since fetuses lack certain psychological properties of personhood (e.g., reason, mentation, consciousness, self-awareness, etc.), it is enough for the pro-choicer to conclude that most abortions (especially early ones) are not wrongful killings. Generally speaking then, each side wants to utilize a governing moral principle that will allow for its particular position to stand as correct.

Abortion and the Ethics of Killing

Upon examining the respective positions, we find that both make a similar move and suffer from a similar difficulty. When pro-lifers claim, "It is wrong to kill an innocent human being," they utilize a biological category to establish their moral standpoint. That is, invoking the biological category of "human being" in reference to the fetus is enough to establish that abortion is morally wrong. When pro-choicers claim, "It is only wrong to kill persons, rational beings, beings with a developed brain stem, etc.," they utilize a psychological category to establish their moral standpoint. That is, the category of "personhood" understood by way of psychological criteria does the job of establishing that most abortions are not im-

The Future of Value Argument

Consider human adults and already born children, about whom a consensus exists that killing them is wrong. How does killing victimize them? It harms them. Killing harms its victims by depriving them of all of the goods of life that they otherwise would have experienced. In other words, killing them deprives them of their futures of value. Their futures of value consist of whatever they will or would regard as making their lives worth living.

The implications of this account of the wrongness of killing for the ethics of abortion are straightforward. Fetuses have futures very much like ours; indeed, their futures contain whatever ours contain and more. Therefore, (given certain defensible assumptions and a few qualifications) abortion is immoral.

The future of value account of the wrongness of killing is superior to the standard account because it appeals to what we actually do believe makes life valuable and what makes premature death a misfortune.

Don Marquis,
"Abortion and the Beginning and End of Human Life,"
Journal of Law, Medicine, & Ethics, *Spring 2006.*

moral. The difficulty comes when either side attempts to defend why its category should make the moral difference. Both seem to rely on circular reasoning, assuming their conclusion in the premise. For example, why should I not kill a human being? . . . because all human life is morally valuable. Or, why should I not kill a person? . . . because being a person (with the capacity to reason, feel pain, etc.) is what gives an individual moral worth. Both sides believe their preferred category to be sufficient by itself to establish their claim about abortion.

Don Marquis, a philosophy professor from Kansas University, wrote an article entitled "Why Abortion Is Immoral," published in *The Journal of Philosophy* [April 1989], proposing a way to avoid the above difficulties. Instead of basing the morality of abortion on either of the above categories, he suggested that we address abortion within the larger discussion of the ethics of killing. That is, before we make any moral decisions about abortion, we should ask: what makes killing wrong in the first place? According to Marquis, killing is not wrong because it shows the killer to be barbaric, nor because it leaves friends and relatives left behind saddened. Rather, killing is wrong primarily *because of the effect it has on the victim.* Killing deprives the victim of life. The loss of one's life is the greatest possible loss anyone can suffer. It "deprives one of all the experiences, activities, projects, and enjoyments that would otherwise have constituted one's future." It is not merely changing the biological state of a victim from alive to dead that it is wrong, but the effect of that change on the victim's future, which forever is taken away. In Marquis' own words: "When I am killed, I am deprived both of what I now value, which would have been part of my future personal life, but also what I would come to value." His conclusion: what makes killing any adult human being wrong is "the loss of his or her future."

The "Future Like Ours" Argument

Marquis adds that this explanation for the wrongness of killing should be preferred if it fits with our natural intuitions about killing and if there is no other better explanation. In addition, he finds his explanation to be supported by several considerations: (1) it explains why many regard killing as one of the worst crimes (i.e., killing is regarded as so horrible because of the great loss it causes); (2) it is incompatible with the view that it is only wrong to kill beings that are biologically human (i.e., it would be wrong to kill any being with a valuable future, like aliens and some animals); (3) it does not necessarily entail that euthanasia is wrong (since those who face an incurable future of pain would not lose a future of value); and (4) it accounts for the wrongness of killing newborns and infants (since they indeed have futures of value like adults).

Thus, if the primary reason for the wrongness of killing is that it deprives one of his or her future, then this has obvious implications for abortion. Every normal fetus, just like you or me, has "a set of experiences, projects, activities, and such which are identical with the futures of adult human beings and are identical with the futures of young children." Since fetuses have a "future like ours," then it follows that abortion is a serious moral wrong. Thus, it is not the category of "being human" or "being a person" that ultimately makes the moral difference in abortion, but the category of having a "future like ours." Just as it would be wrong to arbitrarily kill someone like you or me, since we have valuable futures full of a variety of experiences and enjoyments, it is equally wrong to kill fetuses, because they also have valuable futures. Lastly, under this theory abortion could only be justified if another life (e.g., the life of the mother) was threatened by not aborting.

| "Overturning the ban on abortion . . .
| was a profoundly moral thing to do!"

Abortion Is Not Immoral

Revolution

The debate over the morality of abortion has been at the center of political and social discussions throughout the twentieth century and continues to remain a contentious point. In the following viewpoint, Revolution *newspaper presents the argument that abortion is morally just because women should be able to make the appropriate decisions for their own bodies without the interference of government bans and restrictions. Furthermore, the author maintains that it is immoral to force a woman to carry a pregnancy to term against her will because the pregnancy could be a threat to the mother's health and could result in the birth of a child who is unwanted and who will not receive the proper care.* Revolution *is the official publication of the Revolutionary Communist Party, USA.*

As you read, consider the following questions:

1. According to *Revolution*, what is contraception being equated to today?

Revolution, "The Morality of the Right to Abortion . . . And the Immorality of Those Who Oppose It," March 12, 2006. Reproduced by permission.

2. According to *Revolution*, what is meant by the "whole story"?

3. *Revolution* states that a woman who has no control over her own body is no freer than whom?

The stakes in the battle around abortion are very, very high. These right-wingers will not stop at banning abortion—the end of *Roe v. Wade* would not only be a horror in itself, but would set the stage for even worse. Theocrats like James Dobson and Paul Weyrich have built up a fascist movement by whipping people up against abortion and gay marriage. They won votes for Bush and Senate and House seats for other theocrats in the 2004 elections, and they collected signatures for ballot initiatives to ban gay adoption in the 2006 elections. These victories in banning abortion and gay marriage are only whetting the appetite of religious fanatics who have taken over the Republican Party and been appointed to the highest offices in the land.

Is the Forceful Assertion of Male Domination "Moral"?

There is not a single "pro-life" organization that supports birth control. The mission statement of the largest right-to-life educational organization—the American Life League—reads, "A.L.L. denies the moral acceptability of artificial birth control and encourages each individual to trust in God, to surrender to His will, and be pre-disposed to welcoming children."

The *Pro-Life Activist's Encyclopedia* explains the justification for efforts to ban contraception:

"Contraception cannot be separated from abortion. In fact, anyone who debates on the topic of abortion will inevitably be drawn to the topic of artificial contraception over and over again, especially in the post-*Roe* era of pro-life activism. . . . How does contraception lead to abortion? Quite simply, they are *virtually indistinguishable* in a psychological, physical, and legal sense . . . those individuals [who] use artificial contraception take the critical step of separating sex from procreation. Contraception, *not abortion,* was the first step down the slippery slope."[1]

Banning birth control is the next target of these Christian Fascists. They are already in full swing on this, passing laws in South Dakota, Arkansas, and Mississippi that legally allow pharmacists to refuse to fill birth control prescriptions on moral and religious grounds. And this is becoming the new Christian Fascist litmus test for running for office—in some states, like Kentucky, candidates who want the endorsement of Kentucky's Right to Life must now oppose the use of standard birth control (not just the morning after pill).[2] This lunacy, where contraception is now being equated with genocide, where sex that is not for procreation is evil, and where abstinence is government policy enforced not just here but all over the world, is the ground that politics is now being conducted on.

This is a matter of reactionary religious doctrine in service of a morality that wants to take society backwards. Bill Napoli, a state legislator speaking on behalf of the South Dakota ban on abortion, put it this way: "When I was growing up here in the Wild West, if a young man got a girl pregnant out of wedlock, they got married, and the whole damned neighborhood was involved in the wedding. I mean, they wanted that child to be brought up in a home with two parents, you know the whole story. And so it can happen again . . . I don't think we're so far beyond that, that we can't go back to that."[3]

Napoli's "whole story" is one where young people are *forced*—through the notorious "shotgun marriages"—to get married and where young women in particular are coerced into having children that they do not want. The "whole story" is one of reasserting and reinforcing the traditional order of things where a woman's role is to be subordinate to her husband and the procreator of his children, where women are openly the property of men to be controlled by their husbands. It means going back to a morality that cuts women off from acting in the larger society, contributing all they can to that, and living full lives as productive human beings in every sphere and independent from men. This is the traditional biblical morality that says wives must "submit yourself unto your own husbands as unto the Lord. For the husband is the head of the wife even as Christ is the head of the Church" (Ephesians 5:22-23)—and these people want to return society to a place where THAT standard sets the law of the land. That would be a horror for women and a terrible thing for society as a whole.

The mass access to birth control and abortion has undermined religious doctrine and traditional morality that subordinated women for centuries. Though they are still held down by the underlying social relations of capitalism, this step enabled women to participate much more in every sphere of society—something that after 30 years we may take for granted but is actually a relatively fragile and new idea in this history of human society. And now these people want to rip this away!

Abortion on Demand and Without Apology

The movement for women's liberation that arose in the 1960s and '70s made widely known and accepted the whole idea of abortion on demand. This unapologetic position of women's liberation changed the culture—it changed the ways people thought and changed the quality of human emotions. It shifted the way millions of people viewed reproductive rights and sexual equality, which paved the way for *Roe v. Wade* and the legalization of abortion in 1973. And this was overwhelmingly positive in emancipating the full potential of women and in benefitting all of society in doing so.

Abortion Is Permissible Despite Moral Problems

We can develop a rich account of abortion by focusing on the virtuous Kantian agent [as defined by eighteenth-century German philosopher Immanuel Kant] and her duties to herself. Virtuous Kantian agents recognize the moral value not only of their rational natures, but also (derivatively) of their bodies, its drives, and its emotional predispositions. This recognition infuses their approach to sexuality, pregnancy, and abortion. Abortion involves a frustration of some morally useful sentiments. The moral costs of abortion generate a deliberative presumption against abortion for inclination-based ends. This presumption may be rebutted when the agent's reasons for abortion have to do with such things as physical risks of pregnancy, or conflicts between the demands of pregnancy and agents' significant, morally grounded commitments. Thus, abortion is morally problematic, but often permissible.

Lara Denis,
"Animality and Agency: A Kantian Approach to Abortion,"
Philosophy and Phenomenological Research, *January 2008.*

There is *nothing* immoral about terminating an unwanted pregnancy or removing a clump of cells that have not yet developed into a viable human being from a woman's body. A fetus is not a baby. If a woman doesn't want to continue a pregnancy all the way (for whatever reason), she should have the freedom to end it, safely and easily. There is nothing tragic about it—indeed, the real tragedy lies in the lives of women that are foreclosed and disfigured and even ended by being compelled to have children that they do not want, a tragedy that happens millions of times a day on this planet, with the connivance and support of the U.S. government.

The life of a woman who is forced to continue an unwanted pregnancy is endangered. From the dangers of illegal abortions to the disrespect for her own life, she is harmed and demeaned as a human being. Being forced by society to have a baby when a woman either does not want or cannot care for one is one of the age-old tragedies that are no longer necessary for anyone to have to suffer. But if a woman is not allowed to control her own body, her own reproduction, not allowed to decide whether or not or when to become a mother, she has no more freedom than a slave. This is for the greater good for the health and overall well-being of that woman, whose life we should value and cherish more than that of a partially formed fetus. And for the greater good of humanity—for don't we want a society where *all* forms of slavery are ended?

The morality that *should* be supported and fought for is one that values the rights of women to lead full social lives. It supports social and intimate relations where people respect each other's humanity and flourish together—and not where women are supposedly commanded by "God" to "submit themselves" to men. This morality sees children as a joy to society, and as ultimately the responsibility of all society, while not compelling anyone in any way to have children against their will. It does NOT, as these theocrats do, sanctimoniously shout hosannas to a clump of cells that might someday become a child—while feverishly upholding the murder of real live children in the war being waged by the U.S. in Iraq, and self-righteously dooming literally millions of other real live children, right in the U.S., to lives of deprivation and punishment—in the name of those same traditional values.

In fact, overturning the ban on abortion—a ban which consigned thousands of women a year to death or horrible mutilation, and millions more to humiliation and oppression—was a profoundly moral thing to do! It was and is part of a morality that corresponds to the fundamental interests of the vast majority of people in this society and worldwide. These values are also consistent with communist morality, which in addition to the emancipation of women aims at the elimination of *all* oppressive and exploitative relations among people and the establishment of a freely associating community of human beings. And at the same time, there are many, many people beyond communists who actually yearn for and even strive to live by values that promote and celebrate equality between women and men, and between peoples and nations; that appreciate both diversity and community; that put cooperation over cutthroat competition and the needs of the people over the accumulation of wealth, that oppose imperialist domination, and that cherish and foster critical thinking.

Notes

1. American Life League, "Introduction: The Abortion-Contraception Connection," Chapter 97 of *Pro-Life Activist's Encyclopedia.*
2. "Right to Life Adds Pill to List" (*Cincinnati Enquirer*, April 2002). Original research from Cristina Page, *How the Pro-Choice Movement Saved America: Freedom, Politics and the War on Sex* (New York: Basic Books, 2002), p. 19.
3. *The NewsHour with Jim Lehrer*, "South Dakota Bans Abortion," March 3, 2006.

> *"Somehow 'convenience' and 'comfort' became values more important than the right to life, where a woman can exterminate any chance at life on a whim."*

Abortion Violates Human Rights

Armstrong Williams

In the following viewpoint, Armstrong Williams argues that abortion is a choice women make without careful consideration for the impact that choice could have on society or the rights of the unborn. Williams is disgusted by the fact that many civil rights organizations fight to protect the rights of the oppressed and even the rights of animals, but do nothing to support an unborn human's right to life. He blames modern feminism for devaluing motherhood and the sacrifices parents make to bring new life into the world. Williams is a conservative commentator who has been labeled "one of the more recognized conservative voices in America" by the Washington Post.

As you read, consider the following questions:

1. According to Armstrong Williams, how does modern Western civilization view childbirth?

2. How did the early American feminist Elizabeth Stanton view abortion?

3. What role does Williams believe modern feminism has played in the increased acceptance of abortion in society?

Although the abortion debate has largely been cast in terms of a woman's right to choose whether or not to give birth to a fetus, based on a set of lifestyle and health-related factors, the alarming number of abortions performed each year suggests a different story altogether.

With well over a million abortions performed annually in the United States alone, more than 50 million abortions performed in America since the Supreme Court's landmark *Roe v. Wade* decision [that deemed abortion a constitutional right] 35 years ago, it might appear that abortion has become little more than a routine medical procedure, undertaking little or no real consideration of its true consequences.

Surely, some of the causal factors behind such a choice are understandable within the context of the world we find ourselves facing. With fatherhood and male role models increasingly absent, and rapidly disintegrating family and community networks, it is no wonder that many women feel they cannot raise a child on their own. While, in many countries, pregnancy is considered an honorable contribution to society, in our modern Western civilization, childbirth, especially among women of prime child-bearing age, is seen through the lens of constricted lifestyle and career choices. Women with children are seen as less valuable in the workplace and less likely to succeed in life. Children are viewed, not as our greatest resource leading to a better future for our civilization and the world at large, but as a burden on our individuality and lifestyle.

There Is No Such Thing as Abortion Rights

Abortion is the only example of taking innocent human life which is protected by the Police Power of the State. It has been given a special status as some sort of "super right" in the American culture these days! The current approach is no different than recognizing a so-called "right" to kill three-week-old babies—if the Supreme Court said it was OK. Abortion is simply feticide in a new language intended to make what is evil sound acceptable. On top of this lie, its advocates have also fashioned a "rights language" around it to make it even sound noble. It does not matter. Intentional abortion is evil, plain and simple.

Keith Fournier,
"After Notre Dame: No 'Abortion Rights' Only Human Rights,"
Catholic Online, *May 15, 2009. www.catholic.org.*

Understanding Early Feminists' Views on Abortion

This choice stems from a prism of values that distort the true nature of God-given equality. This view is not restricted to the Western world, but is surprising given the strides we have made over the past century in upholding and advancing the rights of women. The earliest American feminists, Elizabeth Stanton and Susan B. Anthony, equated abortion with slavery as barbaric practices.

Stanton was quoted as saying, "*When we consider that women are treated as property, it is degrading to women that we should treat our children as property to be disposed of as we see fit.*"

Anthony went as far as to refer to abortion as *"child-murder."* These early pioneers of civil rights and women's suffrage found it abominable that either unborn or fully formed human beings could be considered property, to be used and discarded like animals. In fact, when animals are used in a similar manner, PETA (People for the Ethical Treatment of Animals) goes berserk trying to defend the rights of animals. The ACLU (American Civil Liberties Union) often boasts about advocating those without a voice, yet they sided with the women, who once upon a time had no voice, but who has less of a voice than a baby inside her mother's womb? Somewhere along the way, feminism became distorted and turned on the very values that gave rise to it. Somehow "convenience" and "comfort" became values more important than the right to life, where a woman can exterminate any chance at life on a whim. Is that where we want to be as a society, where lives can be used as leverage or in some tragic cases, as revenge?

The Sacrifice of Parents

Equality, whether in gender or societal terms, has been falsely equated with sameness. When America's founders evoked the principle that people are created equal, they did not mean that all people are the same. Rather, they implied that all are equal in the sight of God; that our diversity of talents and perspectives as individuals should be properly valued as contributions to the growth of a great civilization. One need not be the same in order to be treated equally under the law. But this view has been distorted in modern feminism: Rather than urging a re-valuing of the value of motherhood, modern feminists merely sought to become men in dresses, and some seem intent on doing away with those dresses too. In doing so they overlooked the value of the sacrifice associated with motherhood. It should be noted that even under the best circumstances childbirth is an arduous ordeal, fraught with danger. On the other hand, it is perhaps one of the noblest forms of sacrifice that a person can offer to society, and potentially the most rewarding. We ought not to forget that half of society is incapable of undergoing this sacrifice and having the honor of bringing new life into the world. Yes, bearing children is a privilege that half of us are not afforded, and when people who have power use it to oppress others in order to gain more comfort for themselves we usually call them tyrannical. It's highly dubious that the intent of the feminist movement was to create tyrants out of teenagers and young women or their families who force them to vanquish an unborn baby. Motherhood and fatherhood are not a useless burden: They are the basic building blocks of a great nation. Without the sacrifice of parents, nations could not exist.

> "The 'pro-life' movement is not a de-
> fender of human life—it is, in fact, a
> profound enemy of actual human life
> and happiness."

Abortion Does Not Violate Human Rights

Christian Beenfeldt

In the following viewpoint, Christian Beenfeldt makes the case that antiabortionists profess an antihuman argument that violates human rights. The author believes that forcing women to carry unwanted pregnancies enslaves women because such women are no longer free to make decisions about their own bodies without interference from the government. In addition, Beenfeldt states that embryos or fetuses should not be granted rights or be considered equal to the women who carry them because they are not yet fully developed human beings. Beenfeldt writes for the Ayn Rand Institute, which promotes Rand's philosophy of objectivism.

As you read, consider the following questions:

1. According to the author, what would a ban on abortion mean for human life, particularly the lives of women?

2. What analogy does the author use to make the point that embryos are not the same as human beings?

3. In Christian Beenfeldt's view, what is the ultimate justification for the "pro-life" movement?

I cannot project the degree of hatred required to make those women run around in crusades against abortion. Hatred is what they certainly project, not love for the embryos, which is a piece of nonsense no one could experience, but hatred, a virulent hatred for an unnamed object. . . . Their hatred is directed against human beings as such, against the mind, against reason, against ambition, against success, against love, against any value that brings happiness to human life. In compliance with the dishonesty that dominates today's intellectual field, they call themselves 'pro-life.'—Ayn Rand [author and philosopher who emphasizes the rights of the individual over all else]

South Dakota voters have rejected the state's proposed abortion law [in 2006 and 2008]—a law that would have outlawed abortion in virtually every case. The law's supporters claim that its rejection is a blow to "the sanctity of human life." But is it?

The Enslavement of Women

Consider what banning abortion would mean for human life—not the "lives" of embryos or primitive fetuses, but the lives of real, living, breathing, thinking women.

It would mean that women who wanted to terminate a pregnancy because it resulted from rape or contraceptive failure—or because the would-be father has abandoned her—or because the fetus is malformed—would be forbidden from doing so. It would mean that they would be forced to endure the misery of unwanted pregnancy and the incredible burdens of child rearing. It would mean that women would be sentenced to 18-year terms of enslavement to unwanted chil-

Interfering with a Woman's Rights

A potential person must always be given full human rights unless its existence interferes with the rights of Life, Liberty, and the Pursuit of Happiness of an already existing conscious human being. Thus, a gestating fetus has no rights before birth and full rights after birth.

If a fetus comes to term and is born, it is because the mother chooses to forgo her own rights and her own bodily security in order to allow that future person to gestate inside her body. If the mother chooses to exercise control over her own body and to protect herself from the potential dangers of childbearing, then she has the full right to terminate the pregnancy. . . .

It's actually quite simple. You cannot have two entities with equal rights occupying one body. One will automatically have veto power over the other—and thus they don't have equal rights. In the case of a pregnant woman, giving a "right to life" to the potential person in the womb automatically cancels out the mother's right to Life, Liberty, and the Pursuit of Happiness.

Brian Elroy McKinley,
"Why Abortion Is Moral: Abortion Questions Answered,"
The Event Horizon Rider. www.elroy.net.

dren—thereby suffocating their hopes, their dreams, their personal ambitions, their chance of happiness. And it would mean that women who refused to submit to such a fate would be forced to turn to the "back-alley" at a staggering risk to their health. According to a World Health Organization [WHO] estimate, 110,000 women worldwide die each year from such illegal abortions and up to six times as many suffer injury from them.

An Embryo Is Not a Human

Clearly, antiabortionists believe that such women's lives are an unimportant consideration in the issue of abortion. Why? Because, they claim, the embryo or fetus is a human being—and thus to abort it is murder. But an embryo is not a human being, and abortion is not murder.

There is no scientific reason to characterize a raisin-sized lump of cells as a human being. Biologically speaking, such an embryo is far more primitive than a fish or a bird. Anatomically, its brain has yet to develop, so in terms of its capacity for consciousness, it *doesn't bear the remotest similarity to a human being*. This growth of cells has the *potential* to become a human being—if preserved, fed, nurtured, and brought to term by the woman that it depends on—but it is not *actually* a human being. Analogously, seeds can become mature plants—but that hardly makes a pile of acorns equal to a forest.

What can justify the sacrifice of an actual woman's life to human potential of the most primitive kind? There can be no *rational* justification for such a position—certainly not a genuine concern for human life. The ultimate "justification" of the "pro-life" position is religious dogma. Led by the American Roman Catholic Church and Protestant fundamentalists, the movement's basic tenet, in the words of the *Catechism of the Catholic Church*, is that an embryo must be treated "from conception as a person" created by the "action of God." What about the fact that an embryo is manifestly *not* a person, and treating it as such inflicts mass suffering on real people? This tenet is not subject to rational scrutiny; it is a dogma that must be accepted on faith.

The Pro-Life Movement Promotes Human Rights Violations

The "pro-life" movement tries to obscure the religious, inhuman nature of its position by endlessly focusing on the medical details of late-term abortions (although it seldom mentions that "partial-birth" abortions are extremely rare, and often involve a malformed fetus or a threat to the life of the mother). But one must not allow this smokescreen to distract one from the real issue: The "pro-life" movement is on a faith-based crusade to ban abortion no matter the consequences to actual human life—part of what the Pro-Life Alliance calls the "absolute moral duty to do everything possible to stop abortion, even if in the first instance we are only able to chip away at the existing legislation." This is why it supports the South Dakota law, which is the closest the movement has come to achieving its avowed goal: to ban abortion at any stage of pregnancy, including the first trimester—when 90 percent of abortions take place. As the Pro-Life Alliance puts it: "We continue to campaign for total abolition."

The "pro-life" movement is not a defender of human life—it is, in fact, a profound enemy of actual human life and happiness. Its goal is to turn women into breeding mares whose bodies are owned by the state and whose rights, health and pursuit of happiness are sacrificed en masse—all in the name of dogmatic sacrifice to the pre-human.

The result in South Dakota is the only pro-life result.

| *"'Abortion' doesn't do the reality justice, and this is why 'genocide' is the most accurate term we have now."*

Abortion Is a Form of Genocide

Meredith Eugene Hunt

Meredith Eugene Hunt, a pro-life advocate who has worked with groups such as the Genocide Awareness Project and Life Advocates, maintains in the following viewpoint that referring to abortion as a form of genocide is accurate by historical and accepted standards of the word's definition. Hunt identifies the origin of the term "genocide" and concedes that abortion does not fit perfectly with the original use. But Hunt also goes on to explain that recent classifications of genocide have been expanded to include parameters into which abortion would fit. Most importantly, the author states that the term "abortion" does not adequately convey the horrors of the action it is used to describe and that genocide is the only appropriate term in the current vernacular.

Meredith Eugene Hunt, "Abortion Is Genocide by Definition," *Sidelines*, September 27, 2007. Reproduced by permission.

As you read, consider the following questions:

1. Who first coined the term *genocide*, and when did this occur, according to the author?

2. What evidence does the author present to show that the definition of the term *genocide* has expanded in recent years?

3. Even though Meredith Eugene Hunt recognizes that genocide may not be the most accurate term to describe abortion, why does the author believe it is still appropriate to continue using the term?

[The] use of the term genocide in the Genocide Awareness Project [a traveling exhibit that visits college campuses nationwide and uses graphic photo displays to compare modern abortion to historical genocide] is not flippant. Nor is the use of photos of victims of atrocity exploitive when it is done for humanitarian and educational reasons. We respect the people who have suffered, and our intention is to show the fundamental similarities between killing large numbers of born people and killing large numbers of pre-born people. Also, our hope is to sensitize people with regard to various atrocities, including those of genocide. If any legitimate criticism can be made, it would be that we need to update our images to include victims of the genocide in Sudan.

Genocide Through History

Look at the history of the creation of the term: In August 1941, Winston Churchill [prime minister of England during World War II] called the Germans' "methodical, merciless butchery" of Jewish people in occupied Soviet Russia "a crime without a name." Polish-born advisor to the U.S. military Raphael Lemkin gave that kind of crime—the destruction of groups of people—a name when he coined the word "genocide." The word appeared in print for the first time in his

1944 book, *Axis Rule in Occupied Europe*. In this book, Lemkin began by saying, "New conceptions require new terms."

Another significant milestone in genocide awareness was reached when the United Nations [UN] General Assembly adopted the final text of the Convention on the Prevention and Punishment of the Crime of Genocide in 1948. Since then, 140 nations have ratified the Convention. Genocide is viewed as the worst of the worst imaginable crimes called "Crimes Against Humanity." The Convention and the International Criminal Court define genocide as

> any of the following acts committed with intent to destroy, in whole or in part, a national, ethnic, racial or religious group, as such: killing members of the group; causing serious bodily or mental harm to members of the group; deliberately inflicting on the group conditions of life calculated to bring about its physical destruction in whole or in part; imposing measures intended to prevent births within the group; forcibly transferring children of the group to another group.

By the above definition, abortion could have genocidal characteristics, but would not qualify as genocide legally, because unwanted pre-born children as a group are not "national, ethnic, racial, or religious." Of course, an objection is that pre-born children are not human or are not persons. Our graphic photos presented evidence that they are human. Our discussion at the display strongly supported that they are persons. To quickly address this issue, I will say that there is virtual unanimous scientific consensus that an individual human life begins at fertilization. And check any dictionary for the definition of person. Entry number one will be "a human being."

Expanding the Definition of Genocide

And yet consider other legal definitions of genocide. In addition to ratifying the UN Convention, many world states have

Abortion Is a Hate Crime

Some might argue that abortion is not genocide because genocide is a mass "hate crime" and most aborting mothers don't "hate" their unborn children. That may be true (though immaterial) concerning mothers but it certainly isn't true of abortionists and abortion advocates. Margaret Sanger, the founder of Planned Parenthood, declared war on "unwanted" children with her motto, "every child a wanted child." Planned Parenthood of Minnesota/South Dakota, for instance, has run newspaper advertisements which read in part, "Babies are loud, smelly, and expensive. Unless you want one. 1-800-230-PLAN." This hate-filled attack on "unwanted" unborn babies is couched in the language of bigotry. This is the dehumanizing rhetoric of genocide. Substitute for the word "babies" the name of any racial group and every mainstream newspaper in the country would rightly reject this mean-spirited ad.

Gregg Cunningham,
"Why Abortion Is Genocide," Evangelization Station, 2004.
www.evangelizationstation.com.

their own statutes that define genocide in terms differing from the international standard. Some laws are more narrow and some broader.

Amnesty International's Web site lists a dozen states whose laws against genocide either increase the number of protected groups or increase the scope of offenses that qualify as being genocide. Amnesty International sees the development of broader definitions of genocide to be positive. For example, in Ecuador, the number of groups is expanded to include those defined on the basis of political condition, gender, sexual orientation, age, health, or conscience.

The official French definition, while not as specific as Ecuador's, is perhaps the most inclusive of any nation. France's definition of genocide begins with the recognized target groups of "national, ethnic, racial and religious" but adds, "or of a group determined by any other arbitrary criterion."

So it seems that the Genocide Awareness Project is not far afield in expanding the meaning of genocide. In the case of abortion, the group of human beings intended for destruction "in whole or in part" is determined by size, age, degree of dependency, location, level of function and a vague, imposed condition of unwantedness; abortion therefore qualifies as genocide under the French definition, and that of a few other nations, because those criteria are all arbitrary as excluders from the human family.

All this being said, it is not our intent to advocate for abortion to be classed as the crime of genocide. In some respects, a woman who aborts is a second victim. She has grown up in a culture where abortion is legal and generally accepted—where knowledge of the true nature of abortion has been suppressed, where autonomy at the expense of others is celebrated, where sexuality is separated from the begetting and rearing of offspring. Often, because of pressure from parents or the boyfriend/husband, or from other sources, she may feel that she has no other choice. Our use of the word "genocide" in the Genocide Awareness Project to describe the massive (55 million per year) worldwide government-supported destruction of pre-born children points to an evil occurring presently in our own nation and communities—an atrocity with which all of us to one degree or another are complicit.

Because genocide as a word connects to race and by extension to religion, ethnicity and nationality, I recognize that genocide is not a perfect expression for describing abortion, nor is it perfect for many historical occurrences when unthinkably large numbers of people are murdered. However, "abortion" doesn't do the reality justice, and this is why "genocide" is the most accurate term we have now. Until we have a better word, maybe a new and unique word, abortion remains a crime without a name.

> "The relationship between women and their unborn children is not the same as the relationship between Nazis and Jews."

Abortion Is Not a Form of Genocide

Cathleen Kaveny

According to the following viewpoint, Cathleen Kaveny believes that the analogy many pro-life activists use to equate abortion with the Holocaust is inaccurate. Kaveny contends that associating someone with the Nazis in contemporary culture is an insult and not something that invites a person into a serious discussion. She believes that four main differences separate abortion from the Holocaust: intentions of the perpetrators, classification, government involvement, and options available to assist victims. She concludes that if we view abortion in the same way that we view the Holocaust, we miss important factors that display that the relationship of the Nazis and Jews is not the same as that of a mother and her unborn child. Kaveny is a teacher of theology at the University of Notre Dame and a contributor to Commonweal *magazine.*

Cathleen Kaveny, "A Flawed Analogy: Pro-Choice Politicians & the Third Reich," *Commonweal*, June 20, 2008. Copyright © 2008 Commonweal Publishing Co., Inc. Reproduced by permission of Commonweal Foundation.

As you read, consider the following questions:

1. According to Kaveny, how are the categories of "Gypsy" and "Jewish" different than "unborn"?

2. What is the difference between the involvement of the Third Reich in the Holocaust and the U.S. government's dealings with abortion?

3. What "key aspect" are we missing when we view abortion through the "lens of the Holocaust," according to Kaveny?

As the 2008 presidential election cycle heats up, the political and moral rhetoric about abortion is reaching the boiling point. Some prominent pro-life Catholics have compared politicians who support abortion rights to the Nazis, and intimated that Catholics who would vote for such politicians are comparable to citizens of the Third Reich who were indifferent to the plight of those condemned to the gas chambers. Is the analogy that equates the American pro-choice legal regime and Nazi Germany correct? I do not think it is.

Let me begin with a disclaimer. In contemporary American political discourse, associating someone with the Nazis is usually an insult, not an invitation to serious dialogue. But as a teacher of ethics, I have encountered many pro-life students who have grappled with the Nazi analogy in a sincere and even agonized manner. Precisely because they are asking a question, not hurling an insult, they deserve an answer.

Differences Between Abortion and Genocide

One important difference between the Holocaust and the American practice of legalized abortion has to do with the intentions of the perpetrators. The Final Solution implemented the judgment that all Jews (and other targeted populations) were a blight and drain on the German volk. For that reason,

Abortion Rhetoric Is Used to Stigmatize Other Reproductive Technologies

Those committed to a fundamentalist Christian ideology tend to view the topic of abortion broadly, extending its borders to include a variety of reproductive issues that involve early termination of pregnancies or the manipulation and destruction of human embryos. Both early termination of pregnancy and embryo destruction are believed by many evangelicals to be quite literal examples of murder. This view of abortion-related phenomena carries with it a very distinct epistemological approach to reproductive technologies as well as a well-developed inventory of rhetorical devices that can be used to describe these technologies. With 45% of the articles in the Christian fundamentalist news sample explicitly referencing abortion, human cloning has clearly come to be perceived as one such abortion-related technology. As such, cloning has attracted the same type of '*death*' rhetoric that characterizes much of Christian fundamentalists' communication about abortion per se. Over time, repeated use of the conceptual metaphor '*human cloning is abortion*', combined with a strong tendency to view human cloning as a fundamentally religious issue, could establish the long-term rhetorical framework for large-scale political mobilisation of Christian fundamentalists against any form of human cloning technology (including cloning for therapeutic or research purposes). . . .

Eric Jensen and Lisa H. Weasel,
"Abortion Rhetoric in American News Coverage
of the Human Cloning Debate,"
New Genetics and Society, *vol. 25, no. 3, December 2006.*

the goal of the Third Reich was the elimination of "inferior races." No one in the United States argues that unborn children as a class are akin to social vermin—no one is aiming to eliminate or kill all unborn children. U.S. law does not force women to have abortions.

A second difference pertains to the type of classification involved. Nazi racial classifications such as "Jewish" or "Gypsy" are both exclusive and permanent. For the Nazis, some individuals are Jews, others are not. Moreover, it was impossible for an individual to move out of a disfavored category into a favored one. Once a Gypsy, always a Gypsy. In contrast, the category of "unborn" works very differently. It is not permanent: A particular human being remains in the category for at most nine months. And it is a category in which everyone has at one point belonged. So while abortion is intentional killing in many cases, it is not genocide—it does not aim to eliminate "them," a group of people who are deemed totally and permanently different from and inferior to "us."

A third difference concerns the extent of government involvement. The Third Reich directly ordered and carried out the killing of Jews, Gypsies, homosexuals, and other populations. In contrast, the U.S. government does not demand the killing of unborn children in general or of any particular unborn child. Instead, it declines to protect the unborn against one type of private killing initiated by one particular person—the mother. Importantly, it protects the unborn from other kinds of assault. No third party has an independent right to kill an unborn child. The millions of Jews killed in the Final Solution were killed as a direct result of the policy of a ruthless government. In contrast, the millions of unborn children killed since 1973 were killed because of the individual decisions made by millions of women who as a class should be considered more desperate than ruthless.

A fourth difference pertains to the options available for assisting the victims. The Nazis cracked down on anyone who agitated on behalf of the Jews or took steps to help them. In contrast, the pro-life movement in the United States has a strong political voice. Ongoing efforts to convince women to carry their pregnancies to term, and to give those women assistance in doing so, are entirely legal and legitimate, and often effective. Crisis pregnancy centers are not analogous to the "secret annex" in *The Diary of Anne Frank*.

The Treatment of the Unborn Is Not Equal to the Treatment of the Jews

In short, those of us who believe that the unborn are full members of the human community have morally relevant reasons for distinguishing between Nazi Germany's treatment of the Jews and the treatment of the unborn under U.S. law. What follows from keeping those reasons firmly in mind? In my view, two things. First, a continuing commitment to the legitimacy of the U.S. government and its Constitution. I simply fail to see how those who equate the Holocaust with legalized abortion can avoid the conclusion that the U.S. government merits the same fate as the Nazi regime.

Second, if we view abortion narrowly through the lens of the Holocaust, we miss a key aspect of the problem. The relationship between women and their unborn children is not the same as the relationship between Nazis and Jews. Many women who face crisis pregnancies are themselves financially and socially vulnerable. Carrying a baby to term is not a simple matter of refraining from intentional killing; it also requires a positive investment of one's physical and emotional strength. At the end of the process comes an anguishing decision about whether to raise the child oneself or to give it up for adoption. This means that any effective response to the problem of abortion must help vulnerable women find the strength to protect those even more vulnerable than themselves—and find the hope that they themselves can flourish in doing so.

Periodical Bibliography

The following articles have been selected to supplement the diverse views presented in this chapter.

Joseph Bottum	"Abortion After Obama," *First Things: A Monthly Journal of Religion & Public Life*, January 2009.
Judie Brown	"Toward a Personhood Amendment," *New Oxford Review*, February 2009.
William F. Buckley Jr.	"Crime? Punishment?" *National Review Online*, November 19, 2007. www.nationalreview.com.
Christianity Today	"Reducing Abortion for Real," March 2009.
Karen Frantz	"The Politics of Personhood," *Humanist*, November-December 2008.
David Mills	"License to Kill," *Touchstone: A Journal of Mere Christianity*, January-February 2008.
William Saletan	"Three Decades After *Roe*, a War We Can All Support," *New York Times*, January 22, 2006.
Thomas A. Shannon	"A Change in Tone," *America*, February 9, 2009.
Andrew Sullivan	"Life Lesson," *New Republic*, February 2005.

OPPOSING
VIEWPOINTS®
SERIES

CHAPTER 2

Should Abortion Rights Be Restricted?

Chapter Preface

In February 2009, the North Dakota House of Representatives voted 51–41 to approve a measure giving a fertilized human egg the legal rights of a human being. Bill HB-1572 declares that "any organism with the genome of Homo sapiens" is a person protected by rights granted by the North Dakota Constitution and state laws. Representative Dan Ruby sponsored the "Personhood Bill" and said the legislation does not automatically ban abortion in his state, although he had previously introduced bills in legislature sessions to do just that. "This language is not as aggressive as the direct ban legislation that I've proposed in the past," Ruby told the *Bismarck Tribune*. "This is very simply defining when life begins, and giving that life some protections under our Constitution—the right to life, liberty and the pursuit of happiness."

Ruby's sentiments were echoed by another resident and are indicative of how emotionally charged the debate is. "North Dakotans have gotten used to cold temperatures like -44 degrees, but they haven't gotten used to child killing. We applaud and support their efforts to protect every baby by love and by law," said Cal Zastrow in a press release from Personhood USA, a Christian organization. Zastrow and his family worked on the North Dakota bill on the grassroots level.

The bill was defeated in the North Dakota Senate in April 2009 in a 29–16 vote. The move by the North Dakota legislators is part of a new political movement that uses the term "personhood" to define fetuses as full-fledged human beings deserving of all the legal status of a baby, a child, or an adult. The personhood movement is gaining ground across the nation and is influencing legislation designed to emphasize the human traits of fetuses. For example, in May 2009, the Texas Senate passed legislation that requires doctors performing abortions to offer to show the woman an ultrasound image of the fetus and allow the woman to hear the fetus's heartbeat. This bill, SB-182, expands Texas's informed consent law, which initially required women to be informed of the health consequences of abortions. The new legislation, however, does not require the woman to view the ultrasound image if she refuses.

In Wyoming, the Republican Party sponsored two anti-abortion House bills and a third Senate bill. House Bill-151 would require doctors to conduct an ultrasound and describe to a woman the features of her fetus before the abortion. Right to Life, the Diocese of Cheyenne and the WyWatch Family Action supported 151, which was defeated by the Wyoming House Labor Committee in February 2009. The second legislation, Bill-154, would require providers to file an abortion report and include details such as whether the pregnancy resulted from a sexual assault. The Labor Committee also defeated this bill. Finally, Senate File 97 would adjust Wyoming's criminal statutes to include "unborn children" in its definition of crime victims. The Senate Judiciary Committee rejected this legislation, known as the Unborn Victims of Violence Act, though its sponsor, Republican state senator Kit Jennings, vowed to introduce the bill again in 2010.

In the following chapter, commentators discuss whether abortion rights should be restricted and explore how such restrictions, including late-term abortions and parental consent laws, might apply to subjects.

| "*Partial-birth abortion has ... exposed the depravity of late-term abortion and its similarity to infanticide.*"

Late-Term Abortions Should Be Banned

Susan E. Wills

Partial-birth abortion *is a term used to describe an abortion procedure in which a fetus is partially delivered before being aborted. Debate continues as to the correctness of the term; however, Susan E. Wills argues in the following viewpoint that an abortion procedure that allows any portion of the fetus's body to be delivered is wrong and should be banned. Wills provides descriptions of the procedure and testimony from doctors and judges to support her belief that partial-birth abortion crosses a line and is no different than infanticide. The author further contends that American public opinion supports a full ban of this procedure. Wills works as the associate director for education at the United States Conference of Catholic Bishops, Secretariat of Pro-Life Activities.*

Susan E. Wills, "Partial-Birth Abortion: A Bridge Too Far," United States Conference of Catholic Bishops, 2006. Reproduced by permission.

As you read, consider the following questions:

1. To what historical event does Susan E. Wills compare the abortion industry's defense of partial-birth abortion?

2. According to an April 2005 poll cited by the author, how do Americans view abortion?

3. For what three reasons does Wills believe there is hope that the Supreme Court would uphold the ban on partial-birth abortion?

In 1992, Martin Haskell, MD presented a paper called "Dilation and Extraction for Late Second Trimester Abortion" at a National Abortion Federation (NAF) seminar. There he explained the "D&X" abortion method he "routinely" used to kill unborn children at 20- to 24-weeks' gestational age (and sometimes through 26 weeks). Within a year, D&X abortion became known outside the abortion industry. In March 1996, in riveting eyewitness testimony to Congress, a nurse gave "partial-birth abortion" (as it came to be known) a face— specifically the "most perfect angelic face" of a baby boy at 26 1/2 weeks' gestational age. Dr. Haskell had delivered the boy alive, feet-first, up to his neck, then stuck scissors into the base of his skull, inserted a suction tube and vacuumed out his brain.

The abortion industry's defense of this grotesque procedure brings to mind the disastrous Allied attempt to break through German lines at Arnhem. It was the Nazis' last victory on the Western front, resulting in 18,000 Allied casualties. Shortly before the operation, an Army deputy commander had told [British military commander] Field Marshal [Bernard] Montgomery: "I think we may be going a bridge too far."

It's not likely that anyone cautioned Dr. Haskell before he took the stage at the NAF seminar, but partial-birth abortion is undoubtedly the "bridge too far" for the abortion industry.

And while Montgomery's miscalculation of Nazi strength did not change the outcome of World War II, the defense of partial-birth abortion is already undermining the regime established by the U.S. Supreme Court in *Roe v. Wade* [a 1973 Supreme Court case that deemed abortion a constitutional right]. Ultimately, partial-birth abortion may be *Roe's* undoing.

Where to Draw the Line on Abortion

Some have been admirably clear about the nature of partial-birth abortion. The late senator Daniel Patrick Moynihan, for example, called it "not just too close to infanticide; it is infanticide, and one would be too many."

But many others disagree. In philosophical terms, partial-birth abortion is the *reductio ad absurdum* [Latin for "reduction to the absurd"] of the premise that a woman has a constitutional right to have a doctor kill her offspring for economic or social reasons at the earliest stage of pregnancy. Once you accept the premise that the law must allow for living, developing unborn children to be killed, there is no logical end point—not "viability," not 4/5th of the way through delivery, not after the child is born, and not even during the tumultuous toddler and teenage years. In fact, comparing the short-term inconvenience of pregnancy to the very prolonged challenge of living in close quarters with one's teenaged children, one could plausibly argue for extending the abortion license up to, say, the 83rd trimester!

Some judges have *defended* partial-birth abortion on the ground that there is no moral or logical difference between it and the alternative, equally gruesome second-trimester abortion method of dismembering a child in the womb and removing his body parts piecemeal. As Chief Judge Richard Posner of the Seventh Circuit Court of Appeals has stated:

> From the standpoint of the fetus, and, I should think, of any rational person, it makes no difference whether, when the

skull is crushed, the fetus is entirely within the uterus or its feet are outside the uterus. Yet the position of the feet is the only difference between committing a felony [had the states' partial-birth abortion ban become effective] and performing an act that the states concede is constitutionally privileged.

Supreme Court Justice John Paul Stevens seconded this viewpoint in his concurring opinion in *Stenberg v. Carhart*, the 2000 U.S. Supreme Court case which struck down Nebraska's partial-birth abortion ban. Justice Ruth Bader Ginsburg joined him in observing:

> Although much ink is spilled today describing the gruesome nature of late-term abortion procedures, that rhetoric does not provide me with a reason to believe that the procedure Nebraska here claims it seeks to ban is more brutal, more gruesome, or less respectful of 'potential life' than the equally gruesome procedure Nebraska claims it still allows. . . . [T]he notion that either of these two equally gruesome procedures performed at this late stage of gestation is more akin to infanticide than the other, or that the State furthers any legitimate interest by banning one but not the other, is simply irrational.

A Reassessment of Partial-Birth Abortion

Perhaps it *is* irrational to oppose partial-birth abortion and not try equally hard to ban mid- and late-trimester dismemberment abortion. But it was not the pro-life community or the American public that created a law permitting the dismemberment of unborn children in the first place. That policy was foisted on the country by the Supreme Court in its 1973 decisions *Roe v. Wade* and *Doe v. Bolton*, which drew an arbitrary line between human life and (merely) "potential" life at the birth canal.

Doctors who perform late-term abortions have made their view clear—the difference between killing a partially-born child and one who is fully delivered is a legal technicality. Dr.

Mitchell Creinin, for example, testified candidly in 2004, (in a case the U.S. Supreme Court has agreed to review):

> "If I had a fetus at 24 weeks and I had enough dilation to bring it out intact, I would hold it in to perform the act that would kill the fetus." [Commenting on the testimony in closing arguments, a Justice Department attorney observed:] ... "[A]nd so you wonder why Congress concluded that this procedure comes close to infanticide in its practice. Dr. Creinin's testimony is proof of that. A 24-week fetus that could come out might have a chance of survival [and] he would hold it in[,] in order to kill it."

Thanks to eight years of hearings and debates in Congress, pro-life educational efforts, and the proliferation of alternative news sources, particularly the Internet, Americans did learn about partial-birth abortions, and over 70% want to ban them. Dr. Haskell's 1992 presentation has had far-reaching consequences, including the following.

Shifts in American Public Opinion

At least one wire service, one major polling company and a number of major newspapers still misrepresent *Roe* as legalizing abortion only "in the first three months of pregnancy." So for many Americans, the fact that abortions are being done in the second and third trimesters of pregnancy, and are legal for any reason throughout pregnancy, came as shocking news.

The gruesome particulars of partial-birth abortion shifted the focus of the public debate away from the sometimes difficult social and economic circumstances women may face due to an unplanned pregnancy, toward the act itself. Aided by this debate and the growing use of ultrasound, many Americans began to see the child (routinely described by abortion supporters as an insignificant "mass of tissue" or "products of conception"). The child's obvious humanity changed the debate from a woman's "right to choose" to the question: How can *any* circumstances a pregnant woman may face justify killing her child?

As a result of Americans taking a second look at abortion, nationwide polls have recorded a seismic shift toward pro-life positions. From 1991 to 1995, polls showed that 32% of Americans, on average, favored unrestricted abortion. In mid-1996, as public knowledge of partial-birth abortion spread, such support dropped to 25%. In an April 2005 poll by the polling company inc.™, which offered six possible views on abortion's legality, only 10% said abortion should be "legal any time, for any reason." That compared to 17% who responded "never legal," 14% who said "only legal when the mother's life is in danger," and 31% who would permit abortion only when the mother's life is at risk and in cases of rape and incest.

New Opinions Impact Public Life

For years it appeared that journalists had been writing news stories based almost entirely on press releases from [the pro-choice groups] Planned Parenthood and the National Abortion Federation. Initially, some journalists obligingly reported that the partial-birth abortion procedure was extremely rare and performed only in cases of severe fetal anomalies or for serious maternal health reasons. However, skeptical journalists at publications like *American Medical News* [published by the American Medical Association] and the *Record* [a newspaper in Bergen County, New Jersey] did their own research, and discovered that thousands of partial-birth abortions were being done annually, primarily on healthy mothers and healthy babies. Americans began to realize that biased or lazy journalists had not given them the full truth about abortion in general.

The strong public reaction against partial-birth abortion (over 70% in many polls) resulted in the enactment of laws banning the procedure in 30 states between 1996 and 2000. Congressional efforts to ban partial-birth abortion nationwide were stymied by two vetoes by President [Bill] Clinton and, in June 2000, by the Supreme Court when it declared Nebraska's law unconstitutional. Americans saw how some in government can disregard and thwart the will of the people on this issue.

Partial-birth abortion has also had a probable influence on elections. In the 1994 congressional races, not one pro-life incumbent lost his or her seat to a pro-abortion challenger. NARAL Pro-Choice America (NARAL) [National Abortion Rights Action League, a pro-choice organization], in its 2006 report on reproductive rights, identifies twenty-four states as having pro-life legislatures, nineteen of which also have a pro-life governor; the report states that nine states have a majority pro-choice legislature, and only four of them also have a pro-choice governor. A March 2006 poll by Zogby International, polling over 30,000 respondents in 48 states, caused John Zogby to conclude that pro-choice candidates "will have trouble gaining a political advantage by using the emotionally charged issue of abortion," because almost every question elicited a majority or plurality pro-life response.

NARAL's report also describes a flurry of pro-life legislative activity at the state level. Fifty-eight pro-life measures passed in 2005 alone, of the 614 pro-life measures considered that year. Because of this, NARAL gave the nation a grade of D-minus in protecting "reproductive rights."

Public Critique of Abortion

In the past two years, many pro-choice pundits and legal scholars have published scathing analyses of *Roe v. Wade's* legal and political deficiencies. They now recommend that abortion be regulated at the state level, as it was before the Supreme Court's wrenching it away in 1973.

A growing number of federal judges are openly criticizing the Supreme Court's abortion jurisprudence for, among other

Prospects for Overturning *Roe v. Wade*

When Samuel Alito replaced Sandra Day O'Connor on the Supreme Court in 2006, observers predicted that [Justice] Anthony Kennedy would quickly become the key figure in the nation's jurisprudence. And recent terms have confirmed those predictions: Across a wide range of controversial constitutional issues, Kennedy now holds the balance of power on an otherwise deadlocked court—particularly on abortion.

Writing for a 5–4 majority in last June's [2007] *Gonzales v. Carhart,* Kennedy upheld the constitutionality of a federal statute banning the horrific practice known . . . as "intact dilation and extraction" . . . [or] "partial-birth abortion." The result was cause for at least modest celebration, particularly when contrasted with the court's 2000 *Stenberg* decision, in which a different 5–4 majority struck down Nebraska's ban on partial-birth abortions, over Kennedy's dissent.

The decision in *Carhart* was achieved because Kennedy joined forces with Justices [Antonin] Scalia and [Clarence] Thomas (both of whom are open opponents of *Roe v. Wade*) and Chief Justice Roberts and Justice Alito (who haven't committed themselves on *Roe* but are presumably willing to limit abortion rights). For thirteen frustrating years . . . it was O'Connor who played the role of swing justice on abortion, and *Stenberg* was the disastrous result.

Stephen G. Gilles,
"As Justice Kennedy Said . . ." First Things:
A Monthly Journal of Religion and Public Life,
January 2008.

things, unclear and inconsistent standards which often contradict the standards applied in other legal contexts. Among those critical of the Supreme Court's handling of abortion are: Judge Edith Jones of the 5th Circuit Court of Appeals; Judge J. Harvie Wilkinson III and Judge Paul Niemeyer of the 4th Circuit; and Chief Judge John Walker Jr. and Judge Chester Straub of the 2nd Circuit.

Abortion supporters have long urged senators to impose a "litmus test" on judicial nominees, requiring that they demonstrate wholehearted allegiance to *Roe v. Wade*. Because *Roe's* system of abortion on demand throughout pregnancy is not well grounded on the Constitution or public sentiment, preserving it demands the approval of justices who favor that decision. But Americans now strongly disagree with such a litmus test and oppose using a filibuster to keep qualified nominees who are not pro-abortion off the bench. Public opinion against the litmus test and filibuster may well have contributed to the recent Supreme Court confirmations of Chief Justice John Roberts and Justice Samuel Alito, as neither jurist is known for publicly supporting *Roe v. Wade*. And given the disposition they've already demonstrated to decide cases on the basis of what the Constitution actually says, *Roe's* shaky foundations may be in for renewed scrutiny.

Defining Partial-Birth Abortion Specifically

The Supreme Court's 2000 decision in *Stenberg v. Carhart* found Nebraska's partial-birth abortion ban unconstitutional, with the result that state bans in 29 other states were voided. Three federal district courts later found the federal Partial-Birth Abortion Ban Act of 2003 unconstitutional on the basis of *Stenberg*. Three federal appellate courts have agreed (although the decision in the 2nd Circuit was not unanimous). While no one can predict Supreme Court rulings, particularly in the abortion area, there is reason to hope that the Supreme

Court will *uphold* the federal ban on partial-birth abortion when it hears the case of *Gonzales v. Carhart* this fall [2006]. Here's why.

First, the abortion procedure is defined in a more precise and limited way in the federal ban. Nebraska's law prohibited taking an infant's life after a substantial portion of the child's body was delivered into the vagina. In contrast, the federal ban prohibits killing the infant after he or she is delivered "substantially *outside* the mother's body at specified anatomical points"—"in the case of a head-first presentation, the entire fetal head is outside the body of the mother, or, in the case of a breech presentation, any part of the fetal trunk past the navel is outside the body of the mother." There can be no confusion between this procedure and any other abortion method; it is as close to infanticide as it can be.

Second, neither *Roe v. Wade* nor the 1992 decision which affirmed and modified it, *Planned Parenthood of Southeastern Pennsylvania v. Casey*, provides constitutional protection for killing a child who is substantially outside his or her mother's body. Footnote 1 of the *Roe* decision explicitly exempts from that ruling a section of the Texas Penal Code ("Art. 1195. Destroying unborn child") which provides: "*Whoever shall during parturition of the mother destroy the vitality or life in a child in a state of being born and before actual birth, which child would otherwise have been born alive, shall be confined in the penitentiary for life or for not less than five years.*"

Third, when Congress enacted the federal partial-birth abortion ban, it made specific factual findings. Eight years of congressional hearings and debate demonstrated that partial-birth abortion "is never medically necessary" to preserve the mother's health and, in fact, "poses significant health risks" to women. Congress's finding that the ban requires no "health" exception is entitled to judicial deference here as in any other context.

The Possibility of Banning Abortion

Partial-birth abortion has not only exposed the depravity of late-term abortion and its similarity to infanticide. It has also exposed flaws in our legal system which have prevented the American people from stopping this appalling practice. These flaws have prevented the country from protecting unborn children consistent with the Constitution and with the moral aspirations of the American people, guided by the self-evident truths in our Declaration of Independence.

We have learned a great deal about abortion since the *Roe* and *Casey* decisions, not least about the physical and emotional toll it exacts from women. The frustration has been that the facts, the truth, did not seem to matter when it came to abortion. We can hope that the Supreme Court will review *Gonzales v. Carhart* with minds attuned to the Constitution, and hearts open to the truth about human life.

> "[Insisting that late-term fetuses cannot legally be aborted] effectively proclaims that women's vaginas are exterior to their bodies—public rather than private spaces."

Late-Term Abortions Should Not Be Banned

Abortion Rights Coalition of Canada

In the following viewpoint, the Abortion Rights Coalition of Canada maintains that late-term abortions are rare and reserved primarily for women whose health is threatened by the delivery of a fetus. This nationwide political pro-choice organization states that antiabortion activists have been successful in engendering sympathy for late-term fetuses, thus drawing attention away from the fact that women still should have the right to control their own bodies and ensure their own health. According to the coalition, this misinformation campaign needs to be exposed so that women's rights and the laws that permit abortion are not undermined.

As you read, consider the following questions:

1. As the Abortion Rights Coalition describes it, what is a D&X procedure?

2. According to the coalition, how have antiabortion groups tried to get around laws that would permit the abortion of a late-term fetus?

3. Why are federal and state courts overturning laws that ban late-term abortions, as the coalition explains?

"Partial-birth" abortion does not exist; there is no such procedure. The term is not used by the medical profession, and has never appeared in a medical journal. The phrase was invented in 1995 by antichoice strategists in the United States hoping to ban late-term abortions. Many American courts have ruled that their definition of "partial-birth" abortion is so vague it could apply to a range of abortion procedures, including the one commonly used for second trimester procedures—dilation and evacuation (D&E). It is often assumed, however, that "partial-birth" abortion refers to the intact dilation and extraction (D&X) procedure, which is a much rarer procedure reserved for late-second term and third-trimester abortions. D&X is designed primarily to be used in the case of fetuses that are dying, malformed, or threatening the woman's health or life. The procedure involves pulling the fetus from the womb, except for the head which is too large to pass without injuring the woman. The head is then collapsed to allow removal.

Misleading Terms and Imagery

Antiabortion advocates use the term "partial-birth" abortion to create a new category for the fetus as "not unborn." In 1973, the Supreme Court of the United States ruled that a fetus is not a person (*Roe v. Wade*). It did not, however, declare that a fetus in the process of being born is not a person. The main goal of the 1995 act to ban "partial-birth" abortion was to bypass *Roe v. Wade* by granting citizenship to the "not unborn." The 1995 act declared that "the term 'partial-birth abortion' means an abortion in which the person performing the abortion partially vaginally delivers a living fetus before killing the fetus and completing the delivery." This definition potentially impacts a wide range of procedures, for if anything enters the vagina from the uterus before fetal demise—even a small piece of umbilical cord—the fetus is transformed from the category of unborn to that of "not unborn" or "partially born."

The most misleading aspect of antiabortion accounts of "partial-birth" is the insistence that anything passing into the vagina is outside of a woman's body and thus "not unborn." This definition effectively proclaims that women's vaginas are exterior to their bodies—public rather than private spaces. Such misrepresentation of the female body is standard in antiabortion imagery. Ubiquitous photographs of miscarried fetuses, for example, erase all signs of the maternal body to create the fantasy that fetuses are autonomous individuals. Yet in order to convince the public that "partial-birth" abortion is wrong, antiabortion advocates have primarily created and disseminated drawings. A popular antichoice drawing featured on many Web sites purports to depict "A Doctor's Illustrated Guide to Partial-Birth Abortion." Scholar Carol Mason explains that this drawing portrays a healthy, viable, and whole toddler (not a fetus) being removed from a uterus. The pregnant woman lacks all other internal organs, as well as a head, legs, and arms. Her vagina has been entirely erased. This strategic removal of the maternal body allows the viewer to avoid seeing the woman as a person who has made a difficult decision about an unhealthy fetus. It represents the fetus as a child in need of protection, encouraging viewers to identify with it rather than with the pregnant woman. . . .

Who Gets Late-Term Abortions?

Often lost in the debate over D&X [intact dilation and extraction] abortion is the fact that the procedure is exceedingly rare; in 2000, there were just 2,200 cases—or 0.17 percent of all abortions. The procedure is rare because it is used to end a pregnancy late in the second trimester or later, before viability, in a tiny number of cases when the woman's life is in danger. Abortions late in the second trimester are medically involved, potentially risky, painful, and emotionally difficult. So who waits that long?

The answer is simple: women and girls in states of duress. This includes teenagers who didn't realize they were pregnant, or kept hoping they weren't pregnant, or were too frightened to tell anyone and get help (a common plight of incest victims). It also includes women whose pregnancies have gone wrong, such as women found to be carrying fetuses with serious central nervous system anomalies like hydrocephaly.

Christine Stansell,
"Partial Law: A Lost History of Abortion,"
New Republic, *May 21, 2007.*

The U.S. Ban Should Not Stand

On November 5, 2003, President George W. Bush signed into law the Partial-Birth Abortion Ban Act of 2003. Yet over the summer of 2004, judges in three separate federal courts struck down the law, declaring it unconstitutional because it made no exceptions for cases in which a woman's health is at risk. Although the decisions are being appealed to the Supreme Court, a similar legal challenge has already proven unsuccessful—in June 2000, the Supreme Court struck down a Nebraska statute banning "partial-birth" abortion, saying the procedure should remain legal for, among other reasons, the health of the mother. And in 2005, a three-judge panel of the 4th United States Circuit Court of Appeals ruled that a Virginia "partial-birth" abortion ban is unconstitutional because it does not contain a health exception. Antichoice groups oppose most health exceptions because they allow virtually all abortions to remain legal. Since abortion is a health issue, rather than a moral one, it is unlikely the current ban will withstand the legal proceedings designed to overturn it. [Editor's note: In 2007, the U.S. Supreme Court upheld a federal law banning late-term abortions.]

At a policy convention in March 2005, some members of the Conservative Party of Canada attempted to debate a clause calling for a "ban on the performing or funding of third trimester 'partial-birth' abortion." Other Conservatives supported a resolution indicating a future Tory government would "not initiate any legislation to regulate abortion," rendering the "partial-birth" discussion moot. Clearly, the antichoice faction of the party was attempting to mimic antiabortion strategies developed in the United States. This American approach cannot, however, simply be transferred to Canada. No third trimester abortions are done in Canada for "elective" reasons. The Canadian Medical Association's policy is to endorse abortions on request only up to 20 weeks. Hospitals and doctors in Canada comply with this policy. Women who need abortions past 20 weeks for compelling maternal health reasons or serious fetal abnormalities can get them in a few hospitals in Canada, but more often, these women are referred to clinics in the United States (Kansas, Washington State, and Colorado). These out-of-country procedures are generally funded by provincial governments, on the grounds that they are medically required and not easily available in Canada. The lack of availability occurs because later-term abortions require a high level of skill, experience, and dedication, and there are few providers willing or able to do them in Canada. Condemning "partial-birth" abortion or the D&X technique in Canada is simply part of a political effort to promote disinformation about abortion, and to undermine all abortion rights.

| "Well-designed parental-involvement laws have been surprisingly effective at reducing abortion rates among minors."

Parental Consent Laws Are Necessary

Michael New

Michael New is a political science professor at the University of Alabama. He is also the author of a 2008 study for the Family Research Council, which concludes that abortion rates drop when states adopt parental involvement laws. In the viewpoint that follows, New summarizes his findings and the findings of other researchers and reiterates that states requiring parents to be notified if their daughter is seeking an abortion have witnessed a drop in abortion rates among minors. New asserts that parental notification laws are helpful in reducing abortion rates, but that consent laws are more powerful because they ensure parents the right to prevent an abortion to be carried out on their minor daughter, despite the wishes of the minor.

Michael New, "Study Shows Parental Involvement Laws Reduce Abortions from 19-31 Percent," LifeNews.com, September 18, 2008. Reproduced by permission of the author.

As you read, consider the following questions:

1. By what percentage have parental involvement laws reduced abortion in states that have enacted such legislation, as Michael New maintains?

2. According to a 2000 *New England Journal of Medicine* study, how had seventeen-year-olds been evading the parental involvement laws in Texas?

3. As New reports, how many states have enacted two-parent parental involvement laws?

Political candidates who support legal abortion have been changing their rhetoric in recent years. Indeed, during the current election cycle, a number of pro-choice candidates, including Barack Obama, have expressed an interest in lowering the incidence of abortion. Such statements present a unique opportunity for the pro-life movement.

Indeed, pro-lifers should insist that these candidates support pro-life parental-involvement laws. Such laws enjoy broad support and unlike other laws limiting abortion, they can be easily justified as a parental-rights issue. Furthermore, my [2008] study for the Family Research Council provides evidence that well-designed parental-involvement laws have been surprisingly effective at reducing abortion rates among minors.

Indeed, there are a number of academic and policy studies which demonstrate the effectiveness of pro-life parental-involvement laws. Four studies in peer-reviewed academic journals use time-series, cross-sectional data to simultaneously analyze all the enacted pro-life parental-involvement laws over an extended period of time.

These studies find that these pieces of legislation reduce the in-state minor abortion rate by anywhere from 13 to 19 percent. Case studies of parental-involvement laws that have been enacted in Massachusetts, Indiana, Missouri, and Minnesota arrive at similar conclusions about the effects of parental-involvement laws.

Proven Test Cases

However, the best case study of a pro-life parental-involvement law appeared in the *New England Journal of Medicine* in 2006.

This study analyzed the Texas parental-notification law that took effect in 2000. The authors found that the law resulted in statistically significant declines in the abortion rate in Texas among 15-year-olds, 16-year-olds, and 17-year-olds. Now the authors did find some evidence that some 17-year-olds were able to circumvent the law by waiting until their 18th birthday to have an abortion. However, they found little evidence that Texas minors were circumventing the law by obtaining abortions in neighboring states.

My ... Family Research Council study contributes to this body of research.

It is actually the first study that compares the effect of different types of pro-life parental-involvement legislation. The results indicate that parental-involvement laws reduce the minor abortion rate by 13 percent—a finding that is consistent with other research on the subject. However, state laws that require parental consent instead of parental notification are even more effective, reducing the abortion rate by an average of 19 percent. This finding held true for all age groups that were analyzed—17-year-olds, 16-year-olds, and 15-year-olds.

Consent Laws Are More Powerful at Curbing Abortion

There are a number of reasons why parental-consent laws might be more effective than parental-notice laws.

Consent laws, unlike notification laws, would effectively give parents the ability to prevent an abortion from being performed on their daughter. Additionally, a parental-notice law

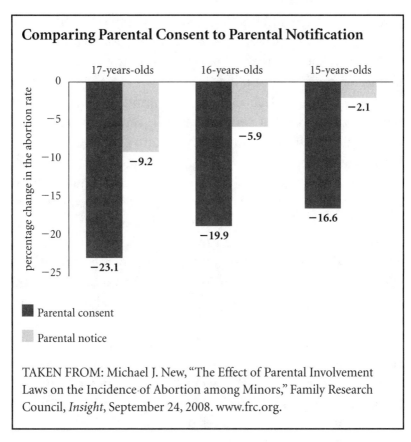

Comparing Parental Consent to Parental Notification

17-years-olds   16-years-olds   15-years-olds

percentage change in the abortion rate

−9.2

−5.9

−2.1

−16.6

−19.9

−23.1

■ Parental consent

░ Parental notice

TAKEN FROM: Michael J. New, "The Effect of Parental Involvement Laws on the Incidence of Abortion among Minors," Family Research Council, *Insight*, September 24, 2008. www.frc.org.

might not deter a minor who feels she can intercept the notification. Finally, it should also be noted that abortion providers might have a greater incentive to follow parental-consent laws. A missed notification can possibly be blamed on timing or other incidental factors. However, failure to obtain consent would likely be seen as the responsibility of the abortion provider and could result in legal action—especially if the parents did not approve of the abortion being performed.

Interestingly, those parental-involvement laws that require the involvement of two parents instead of one are even more effective.

The regression model indicates that these laws reduce the minor abortion rate by 31 percent. Now only three states—Minnesota, Mississippi, and North Dakota—have enacted parental-involvement laws that require the involvement of two parents. However, the substantial abortion declines that have occurred in each of these states suggest that they are models that other states should follow.

These abortion declines all sound impressive. However, it is entirely possible that some of these in-state abortion reductions could be offset by minors who obtain abortions in neighboring states where the laws are more permissive.

Federal legislation has been introduced that would considerably strengthen these state-level parental-involvement laws. The Child Custody Protection Act that has been introduced in the U.S. Senate and the Child Interstate Abortion Notification Act (CIANA) that has been introduced in the U.S. House would make it a felony for anyone other than a parent to take a child across state lines for the purpose of obtaining an abortion.

CIANA and the Child Custody Protection Act passed the House and Senate respectively in 2006. However, this legislation ultimately was defeated when Senate Democrats refused to appoint members to a conference committee to work out the differences in the two pieces of legislation.

Regardless, by making it more difficult for a minor to obtain an abortion in neighboring states, these federal laws could considerably strengthen the state-level parental-involvement laws that are already in place. Indeed, both CIANA and the Child Custody Protection Act should both remain a high priority for pro-life organizations working on federal legislation.

Work to Be Done

Meanwhile at the state level, the pro-life movement still has plenty of work to do.

Right now about 36 states have pro-life parental-involvement laws in effect. However, about 15 of these laws only require parental notification. Furthermore, only three of these laws mandate the involvement of two parents. Strengthening these state laws could be a worthwhile project for pro-life activists. The Supreme Court has consistently upheld strong state-level parental-involvement laws, and it is certainly possible that other legislative proposals to limit abortion at the state level may not withstand judicial scrutiny.

During the 2008 election campaign, abortion will undoubtedly continue to be a major issue. The Supreme Court appointments by the next president will likely determine the extent to which federal government and the states are able to protect unborn children. It is laudable that a number of candidates have expressed an interest in lowering the incidence of abortion.

However, serious pro-life voters should support only those candidates who have a consistent track record of supporting pro-life legislation. While campaign rhetoric often does not amount to much, this study—and other studies—provide solid evidence that well-designed laws are effective at protecting mothers and their unborn children.

> *"Because of parental involvement laws, reproductive options are not a reality for teens whose parents seek to punish their behavior rather than support or protect them."*

Parental Consent Laws Are Unnecessary

Diana Philip

In the following viewpoint, Diana Philip argues that laws requiring parental involvement in a minor's decision to have an abortion are detrimental to the welfare of those young women. In Philip's opinion, such laws force minors who are not ready for the financial or emotional responsibility of parenthood to forfeit the right to decide whether to carry through with an unplanned pregnancy. Philip believes this is a challenge to women's reproductive rights and a form of punishment inflicted on minors who may not agree with their parents' views on abortion. Philip is the cofounder of Jane's Due Process, an organization providing legal services to pregnant minors in Texas.

Diana Philip, "Legal Child Abuse: The Harm of Parental Involvement Laws," Center For American Progress, June 17, 2005. This material was created by the Center for American Progress, www.americanprogress.org.

As you read, consider the following questions:

1. As Diana Philip reports, what percentage of Texas minors involved their parents in the abortion process before the passing of the 2000 parental involvement law?

2. Why does Philip consider the waiver needed to bypass parental consent another obstacle for teens seeking abortions?

3. What are "Baby Moses" laws, according to the author?

No one wants to see a teenager be trapped by poverty, abuse, or neglect. Yet, laws concerning the rights of pregnant minors to access certain medical care do just that.

Since the late 1970s, state legislatures have been passing state "parental involvement" laws, which mandate that a parent or legal guardian be notified of or give consent for a pregnant minor's decision to seek an abortion. Texas has one of the most recent laws, now five years old [in 2005], and as of June 5, 2005, its law changed from requiring notification to mandating consent. Congress is now in the process of creating a nationwide parental notification law through the Child Interstate Abortion Notification Act (CIANA). CIANA also would make it illegal for anyone to help a teen obtain an abortion in another state without satisfying her home state's law. Supporters of this bill generally think such a law will protect children. However, before the Senate votes on CIANA or similar legislation, lawmakers should carefully consider the damage parental involvement laws have done to pregnant youth in Texas.

Overcoming Obstacles in Texas

Mandated notification by Texas clinics did not result in an increase of actual parental involvement in teenagers' decisions regarding abortion, as the law intended. Instead, the state's parental notification law targeted youth whom some lawmakers claim they did not intend to harm. Before the law's enactment in January 2000, Texas abortion providers reported that 80–95 percent of minors involved a parent in the decision to terminate a pregnancy. The ones who did not had compelling reasons. For instance, some parents physically abused, abandoned, or disowned their daughters when they found out they were pregnant. These youth understood that a family that is unable to communicate due to a significant degree of dysfunction, separation, and/or abuse is unlikely to respond appropriately during such an important life decision.

If at least one parent cannot or will not give written consent to the clinic, a minor may seek a judicial bypass waiver by demonstrating that she is mature enough to make the decision, that the abortion would be in her best interest, or that notification will lead to physical, sexual, or emotional abuse. However, although Texas has had over five years to implement a fair system, minors seeking judicial bypass still experience challenges in locating effective counsel and struggle with confidentiality and due process issues in local courthouses. Judges have been known to deny waivers even when the petitioner has met more than one of the three alternative grounds that qualify for a waiver. If the waiver is denied, the minor has a right to appeal. However, when a minor seeks legal relief through the courts, her abortion procedure is delayed, increasing the costs, and at times, the risk of complications in terminating a pregnancy at a more progressed stage. For these and other reasons, some youth consider seeking abortion services out of state, in Mexico, or under unsafe and illegal circumstances.

Desperate Teens and Trying Circumstances

No population of minors is exempt from this law. Not teens removed by the state from their homes for family violence. Not victims of sexual assault whose parents would not believe they were raped and would force them to continue the preg-

Judicial Bypass Is Often Not an Option

For many teenagers living under parental involvement laws, the prospect of going to court for a "judicial bypass" of the parental involvement requirement is daunting or futile. Some teenagers live in regions where the local judges simply never grant bypass petitions. For example, the director of an Indianapolis women's clinic told the *New York Times* in 1992 that she was not aware of any teenager who had been granted a judicial bypass in that city in the prior six years. Other young women have reason to fear being recognized in local courthouses. Still others simply cannot face revealing intimate details of their lives to a series of strangers in a formal, legal process. As the Supreme Court has noted, "The court experience produce[s] fear, tension, anxiety, and shame among minors."

American Civil Liberties Union,
Memorandum on Opposition of the Teen
Endangerment Act (4.R.476), August 30, 2001.

nancy as a punishment for "youthful indiscretion" or due to certain religious beliefs. Not teens who have already given birth and are either active parents or have given babies up for adoption in the past, some forced to do so by their parents. Not orphans or other youth whose parents are missing or incarcerated. All minors must find ways to comply with this very harmful law.

In the last few years, problems have grown regarding pregnant youth along the Mexican border, which some activists have attributed to Texas's parental involvement statutes. Despite the passage of a "Baby Moses" law, which allows a mother to leave her newborn infant at designated safe havens like hospitals or churches without legal repercussions, the number of abandoned infants has risen, resulting in their deaths and the prosecution of their teen mothers. More minors have sought second trimester procedures after illegal ones obtained over the border earlier in their pregnancies failed. And there have been increased reports of abnormalities in infants born to immigrant teens along the border. When tests were run to see if the babies had been affected by environmental causes such as water pollution, medical professionals found that 25 percent of the babies were the result of incest.

A Form of Neglect and Abuse

Mothering with dignity? Becoming a parent when emotionally, physically, and financially ready? Not for these youth. Deciding when to become a parent or whether to have another child has been taken out of their hands entirely. Because of parental involvement laws, reproductive options are not a reality for teens whose parents seek to punish their behavior rather than support or protect them. Just like in any other domestic violence dynamic, the decision to make a teen bear a child against her better judgment is more about power and control than anything else. Where is the dignity in becoming a parent amid domestic violence, sexual assault, and economic abuse? In essence, states have passed laws that allow parents to abuse their daughters and neglect their emotional health. And now Congress wants to do the same.

Periodical Bibliography

The following articles have been selected to supplement the diverse views presented in this chapter.

R. Alta Charo	"The Partial Death of Abortion Rights," *New England Journal of Medicine*, May 24, 2007.
Gregory D. Curfman et al.	"Physicians and the First Amendment," *New England Journal of Medicine*, December 4, 2008.
Caroline de Costa	"Abortion Law, Abortion Realities," *James Cook University Law Review*, 2008
Wanda Franz	"Let Common Sense Prevail," *National Right to Life News*, June 2008.
Kim Gandy	"Not Just Semantics," *National NOW Times*, Winter 2007.
Carole Joffe	"The Abortion Procedure Ban: Bush's Gift to His Base," *Dissent*, Fall 2007.
Frances Kissling and Kate Michelman	"Long *Roe* to Hoe," *Nation*, February 4, 2008.
Dahlia Lithwick	"The Abortion Wars Get Technical," *Newsweek*, December 15, 2008.
Katha Pollitt	"The People's Choice," *Nation*, December 8, 2008.
John Yoo	"Partial-Birth Bigotry," *Wall Street Journal*, April 29, 2007.

OPPOSING
VIEWPOINTS®
SERIES

CHAPTER 3

How Does Abortion Impact Society?

Chapter Preface

Missouri governor Matt Blunt announced in 2007 that he would form a "Task Force on the Impact of Abortion on Women." The task force was not objective. Every appointed member was opposed to legalized abortion and had been chosen for that reason. Blunt declared, "I certainly would begin with the presumption that abortion has a negative impact on Missouri children, Missouri women, Missouri men, because it's harmful to society." The aim of his task force, then, was to discover ways to minimize the damaging psychological, physiological, and social effects of abortion so that proper legislation could be enacted to redress these supposed dangers.

Twenty years before Blunt set up his task force, President Ronald Reagan asked U.S. Surgeon General C. Everett Koop to determine what the effects of abortion were on American women's health. Both Reagan and Koop were pro-life and against legalized abortion. After eighteen months of study, with a large staff to conduct interviews and collect and sort information from over 250 scientific studies, Koop had to admit that the task was impossible. The hundreds of studies, he said, had errors or used different processes, so that the information in them could not be fairly compared. Many papers gave no follow-up information on the patients, and at least half of the women interviewed did not want to discuss whether they'd had an abortion. In the end, Koop told the president and Congress, "We could not prepare a report that could withstand scientific and statistical scrutiny." He went on to say, "There has never been a statistically viable prospective study on a cohort of women of childbearing age that would yield information on the effects of abortion on women."

Whether Koop's assessment is correct, various groups continue to draw connections between abortion and women's health. On the other end of the spectrum from Blunt's task force, Planned Parenthood claims there are benefits to women's health because early-term abortion is accessible. "If safe, legal abortion were not available, more women would experience unwanted childbearing, and unwanted childbearing affects the entire family. Mothers with unwanted births suffer from higher levels of depression and lower levels of happiness than mothers without unwanted births." They point out that genetic diseases can be controlled through abortion and that unwanted children affect whole families in negative ways, increasing poverty and dependence on welfare. Finally, Planned Parenthood notes that in states with the most restrictive abortion laws, women make less money and are not as well educated as women in states with more liberal laws. Also, restrictive states spend less money on children's services such as schools, health care, and foster care.

The essays in the following chapter target the impact of abortion on society. The debates on the issues discussed in these viewpoints and on innumerable other facets of life that are influenced by legal abortion will no doubt continue.

> *"Abortion ... [is] a cancer on American society, eating away at the values and moral principles that have sustained this country for two hundred years."*

Abortion Harms American Society

Daniel W. Kucera

Daniel W. Kucera is a retired Catholic archbishop. In the following viewpoint, Kucera argues that pro-abortion laws and the mind-set that supports them are dangerous to the moral fabric of America. In Kucera's view, abortion is both a result of and, in part, responsible for a foregrounding of self-centered thinking over a concern for the value of others in modern American life. He believes this attitude has cheapened Americans' opinions of life, encouraged people to ignore their responsibilities, and made them less willing to stand up for their convictions. Kucera maintains that Americans must fight for their moral principles to rid society of abortion and other ills that reject life and the values on which the nation was founded. Kucera now serves as a visiting professor of education at Benedictine University in Illinois.

Daniel W. Kucera, "Abortion and the Unraveling of American Society," *Priests for Life*.

As you read, consider the following questions:

1. Why does Daniel W. Kucera believe that individualism in America can be taken too far?

2. On what two "agencies" are Americans becoming too dependent, in Kucera's view?

3. According to Kucera, how are the terms "pro-life" and "pro-choice" being mishandled by the media?

A mong the issues which divide our nation today, that of abortion is surely one of the most troublesome. Almost daily we hear arguments on one side or the other. Crowds demonstrate and politicians debate. Many grow weary of it all, close their ears against the torrent of words and wish the problem would just go away. In such an atmosphere, is it worthwhile to speak out one more time? Will more words make any difference?

But the problem will not go away. We must speak. In fact, the situation grows steadily worse in ways that go beyond the sad fact of abortion itself. Such an important social policy as this cannot have narrowly limited effects. The fact of widespread abortion and the attitudes it encourages have a profound impact on the moral consciousness of our society. We must face that impact and ask just what kind of society we really want. The question is especially urgent as elections approach and we determine who should be entrusted with public office.

Much has already been written from a religious and theological perspective about abortion. These reflections, rather, will focus on abortion as a cancer on American society, eating away at the values and moral principles that have sustained this country for two hundred years. . . .

Individualism and Social Conscience

Americans traditionally pride themselves on being "rugged individualists." Whatever its origins, this trait has in many ways served us well. It has often been accompanied by such values as responsibility, autonomy and personal productivity. Like all human traits, however, in its extreme form it becomes a severe liability. The line between healthy individualism and self-centeredness is all too easily blurred. One consequence is the steady erosion of the sense of social responsibility. This unhappy development is evident today throughout our social structure. . . .

In the midst of this, civil libertarians exert great energy in the defense of individual rights. A Supreme Court justice, now retired, once counseled activists, in view of the increasingly "conservative" complexion of the high court, to turn their attention to state constitutions as untapped sources for the extension of individual liberties, as if the entire purpose of courts and laws were to maximize individual freedom, defined as the absence of social restraint.

What is most insidious about these attitudes is that they contain such a large element of truth. We do need to take care of ourselves. Self-affirmation and a good self-image are essential. Public institutions must not be allowed to oppress the individual. Society must assure a wide range of opportunity for each member. But there is the matter of balance. Laws and institutions are established to mediate between individual rights and the public welfare. Many feel that we are rapidly losing this balance. The sense of social responsibility is in decline. Governments and institutions are thought to exist only to maximize individual advantage while the concept of the common good is ignored.

It would be foolish to assert that an abortion policy is totally responsible for this state of affairs. But thoughtful citizens must ask to what extent that policy grows out of and reinforces our almost pathological individualism. Despite all the rhetoric about health, the poor, rape and incest, it is clear that a substantial percentage of abortions are performed for reasons of personal convenience. What is at stake is often *my* career, *my* earning power, *my* leisure time, *my* material advantages. It is no accident that the "right" to abortion was found in the right to privacy. To make that dubious connection palatable, abortion advocates have contrived to slice the first few months off the continuum of human development and treat individuals in that stage as non-persons.

Devaluing Life

It might seem at first glance that a lessening of respect for life could not be a social tendency linked to abortion since those who support that procedure reject, however mistakenly, the very idea that a human life is involved. This would be a welcome conclusion if it would bear up under close scrutiny. Unfortunately, it does not.

Consider that the rhetoric of "pro-choice" advocates studiously avoids the issue of life. Various subterfuges are used in an attempt to focus on other aspects of the debate which are proclaimed to be the "real" issues. In any argument, when one side pointedly ignores a statement which the other side repeatedly affirms, it is usually evidence of a bad conscience. It is possible that many "pro-choice" people are not really convinced of the non-human character of the unborn child. If this is so, we have a situation of massive self-deception touching on the very sacredness of human life. The willingness to act in such dubious circumstances does not speak well for the future of our nation's respect for life at any stage.

That such doubt must exist flows from the very logic of the situation. Arguments for abortion logically apply throughout the course of pregnancy. It is therefore impossible to see why the termination of a child's life just before delivery differs morally from the same act ten minutes after delivery. Does personhood magically arrive with the severance of the umbilical cord? Reason dictates that if humanity is denied at any given stage in the continuum, we are left to wonder when it does become present. Clearly, once conception has occurred, if we make human personhood dependent upon any qualifications at all, we open up chilling possibilities for the future. The import of this precedent, so thinly disguised with specious arguments, cannot be lost on the general conscience of the public.

There is yet another way in which an abortion mentality works to erode our attitudes toward life. Many of the arguments which claim to champion the poor are "quality-of-life" approaches which embody highly questionable values. Efforts to abolish the suffering caused by poverty must be applauded and supported. But sometimes we hear that if an unborn child will lack certain material advantages, it would be better to prevent that child's birth. Besides its disregard for life as such, this opinion implies that the value of a life is to be measured in material terms. By such standards we would have to conclude that millions of our fellow citizens should never have been born. What does this say about our concept of the purpose of life and our notions of human fulfillment?

This whole complex of attitudes toward life and its purposes can easily lead to programs of eugenics and euthanasia characteristic of tyrannical governments. Indeed, voices in favor of such programs are already heard in our land.

Escape from Responsibility

Increasingly, our society is encouraging dependence on other agencies as a substitute for conscientious social responsibility in the population at large. The two principal surrogates are technology and government.

Abortion is part of a whole complex of attitudes which fosters dependence upon technology to deliver us from the consequences of our own actions. We need do nothing about pollution of the environment for science will come to our rescue. We can smoke, drink, take drugs, overeat and neglect our health because medicine will take care of us. We can conduct our sex lives without thought or responsibility because when all else fails we can always abort, safely, easily and with public support.

Government, too, can be structured in such a way that it will take care of us when we might otherwise have to take responsibility for our own behavior. While the weighty matters of health, education, housing and jobs are neglected, while Congress sits impotent in the face of a crushing national debt, crumbling infrastructure and a deteriorating environment, we grow daily more vociferous in our demand that government provide all of us with the means to avoid the consequences of our own self-indulgence. As such attitudes undermine social institutions we slip toward chaos. The insecurity and fear which accompany a society in chaos will inevitably produce an infantile yearning for a firmer governmental hand. Thus do chaotic societies become fertile ground for the rise of dictatorships, whether of the right or of the left. Freedom understood as unbridled indulgence gives way to that "escape from freedom" which is the pathological desire for order at all costs. Big Brother is in the wings, awaiting our call.

Sacrificing Political Integrity

Any critique of contemporary American politics must start with the voters. While we demand more and more of government, we refuse to get involved, fail to vote and, when we do vote, consider only our own narrow interests. Such attitudes encourage and support the deterioration of political integrity among officials and candidates.

Seeing these attitudes and wanting to keep their jobs, political candidates are tempted to turn to interest-groups, PACs [political action committees] and the 20-second sound bite. The democratic process continues to erode. Government is up for sale to the highest bidder. We look long and hard to find candidates who combine personal integrity, the desire to serve

Deep Differences in Opinion Over the Availability of Abortion

| | Abortion shoud be... | | | | |
	Generally Available	More Limited	Illegal Except Rape/Incest/ Save Mother	Never Permitted	Don't Know
All	35	23	31	9	2=100
Men	34	24	32	8	2=100
Women	35	21	31	11	2=100
College graduate	46	22	24	7	1=100
Some college	33	28	29	9	1=100
High School or less	29	22	37	10	2=100
Conserv Repub	13	15	49	22	1=100
Mod/Lib Repub	31	33	35	1	0=100
Independent	41	27	25	6	1=100
Mod/Cons Dem	34	25	31	8	2=100
Liberal Democrat	64	16	15	3	2=100
White Protestant	26	22	40	11	1=100
Evangelical	14	17	53	15	1=100
Mainline	41	30	23	5	1=100
White Catholic	31	23	32	11	3=100
Secular	60	23	13	3	1=100
Attend church					
Weekly or more	18	19	43	18	2=100
Sometimes	39	25	30	5	1=100
Seldom or never	53	27	16	2	2=100

TAKEN FROM: Pew Research Center, *Abortion and Rights of Terror Suspects Top Court Issues: Strong Support for Stem Cell Research,* August 3, 2005.

and an understanding of leadership in office. Politicians posture instead of telling the truth and the public becomes yet more cynical about it all.

Abortion policy becomes symptom and symbol of this sorry state of affairs. Good people on both sides of the issue are increasingly aware that their convictions are being cynically manipulated for the sake of votes. Of course, there are candidates and office-holders whose private convictions and public efforts coincide. Whether we agree [with] them or not, we must at least respect these few for their integrity.

Candidates who try to have it both ways say, "I'm personally opposed to abortion but don't want to impose my view on others." The ploy is so transparent that it is amazing how effective it can be. Every such candidate for office should be subjected to one simple question: "Just exactly *why* are you personally opposed to abortion?" There can be only one reason. The infant in the womb is a human being. If the infant in the womb is not a human person, there is no reason on earth to object to aborting it. If, then, you are "personally opposed," you must think that unborn is a human person. In the face of that conviction and in the knowledge that over a million human persons are slaughtered each year, you can only come up with a lame unwillingness to "impose your view"?

Unfortunately, the political scene in the country is becoming a vast patchwork of closed ideologies. Instead of submitting specific issues to tests of reason and compassion, people tend to accept a given "party line" in its entirety. Why is it not possible, for example, to be *for* social welfare, peace and the environment and *against* abortion? *For* prenatal life *and for* the authentic liberation of women?

Here it is appropriate to pause for a word to Catholics. Why do some of us feel that if we are opposed to abortion, we must also espouse every extreme right-wing idea that comes along? And why do some of us work hard for peace, justice and liberation but [fall] strangely silent when the topic of abortion arises? Is it so important that our "liberal" or "conservative" friends find our ideological credentials without blemish? Can we not judge issues on their own merits without yielding our minds and hearts to some party line?

Media and Entertainment Biases Abound

On the topic of abortion, the media of social communication in our society have clearly chosen their stance. By and large, dramatists, reporters, editors, talk show hosts and even comedians are solidly in the "pro-choice" camp. This has several unfortunate results.

First of all, those who question present abortion policy find it nearly impossible to get their message effectively before the public or have it reported objectively. The editorial policy of most newspapers supports abortion. Pundits and opinion-makers rarely question the assumption that our present policies are good for society as a whole. But the matter goes far beyond editorials and opinion columns. A . . . study conducted by journalists themselves concluded that, by and large the news media are indeed biased in their reporting on the abortion issue. Supposedly objective reports of meetings, debates and demonstrations are frequently slanted toward the "pro-choice" side. Even the vocabulary of journalists reveals this bias. Those who favor present abortion policies are usually called "pro-choice" while there is a consistent refusal to call their opponents "pro-life." Admittedly, using the terms "pro-abortion" and "pro-life" would indicate the opposite bias, but fairness would dictate that both groups be called by the name they themselves use. This may seem a small matter, but since the terms themselves embody an argument, it is discriminatory to accept the one and not the other. Both sides are clearly "for" one thing and "against" another and wish to be known for the positive aspects of their respective positions.

The situation is similar in the fields of drama and entertainment. Casual remarks or entire dramas may center on the anguish of pregnant women and the "injustice" of denying them the opportunity to escape their suffering through abortion. How often do we see on TV or in films a courageous choice made on behalf of the life of the preborn? How often is the physical and psychological damage of abortion honestly portrayed?

That whole wider complex of attitudes and tendencies described above is also supported and reinforced by the powerful entertainment industry of our nation. Through films, TV shows, commercials and popular songs, we are subjected to a constant barrage of propaganda which glorifies materialism and narcissism. Sex is a commodity used to help sell other commodities. Casual sex without commitment is made the norm and held up for admiration.

Many of the same people who profit from this industry then adopt a self-righteous pose and agitate for contraception and abortion as solutions to the problem of teenage pregnancy which they themselves help foster.

All attempts to redress this situation are hamstrung by the nearly fanatical American devotion to freedom of expression. The sacredness of that concept and its necessity for a free and democratic society are undeniable. But when will we begin to seek ways to preserve that freedom and at the same time demand some social accountability from those relatively small groups which control nearly all the available means of mass communication?

Recent news stories reveal the contradictions in which we are trapped by our notions of free expression. Detailed and intricate laws ensure that not a single penny of the public treasury is used to promote religion in any way. Children in religious schools must move to "safe" public rooms for remedial reading. Only Santas and reindeer are permitted on public school bulletin boards during "winter holidays." Yet if someone wishes to degrade human sexuality or ridicule religion and blaspheme its most sacred symbols, not only may he do so in the name of free artistic expression, he may receive a government grant to assist him. Thus, through their taxes, the very people whose most cherished beliefs he assaults are obliged to pay him to do it. Oppose this and you are denounced as favoring censorship. Perhaps we should claim that religion is only a form of artistic expression (many atheists would agree) and ask for government grants to support catechism classes!

In the face of all this, the effort to teach and promote a way of living which will be respectful of human life in all its aspects is a monumental struggle. Individuals, groups and especially churches which are engaged in that struggle are met with the fiercest resistance while their efforts are vilified and condemned. Editorials and opinion columns make sure that Americans maintain their historic fear of the power of the Church while they are lulled into complacency by the very powers which actually control their minds and hearts. . . .

Taking a Stand

Our struggle against the practice of abortion as such must continue, but that is not nearly enough. If abortion policy expresses and reinforces a whole complex of perilous social trends, we must take a resolute stand against them all. It will not do for Christians to oppose this or that aspect of a sick society while endorsing and lending their supports to others.

Broad tendencies require broad remedies. We are called today to nothing less than a counter-cultural revolution. We need individuals and large groups of Christians who will speak out and, above all, live out a consistent ethic opposed to all destructive social tendencies. We must join together to discuss these issues and to support one another in the construction of thoroughly pro-life ways of thinking and behaving. Our very lifestyle must become a radical rejection of self-centeredness, hypocrisy and consumerism.

Historians have noted that the Christian Church seems to flourish in times of persecution, when its members draw together in solidarity against implacable foes. By contrast, when the Church is unopposed or even wielding political power, zeal and devotion grow cold. The present and future struggle for a truly human society promises to be a campaign worthy of our greatest efforts. If we can be faithful to life in the midst of this struggle, history may well rate these times among the Church's finest hours.

> *"The only thing that laws against abortion do is make abortion dangerous, turn most women into criminals, produce millions of disadvantaged children, and create wide disrespect for the law."*

Abortion Benefits Civilized Society

Joyce Arthur

Joyce Arthur is a pro-choice activist and writer living in Vancouver, Canada. In addition to writing, Arthur edits and publishes Pro-Choice Press, *Canada's only national pro-choice publication. In the viewpoint that follows, Arthur asserts that countries with strict antiabortion laws are plagued with social problems including a low regard for women's rights and health and a disregard for children's welfare. She maintains that nations that allow abortion typically favor women's rights, are concerned with family planning, and encourage personal responsibility for sexual behavior. Arthur believes that these pro-choice policies are hallmarks of a truly civilized government and an enlightened populace.*

Joyce Arthur, "Legal Abortion: The Sign of a Civilized Society," *Pro-Choice Action Network*, October 1999. Reproduced by permission.

As you read, consider the following questions:

1. What impact does Joyce Arthur say antiabortion laws have had on Romania's children?

2. To what does Arthur attribute the declining abortion rate in the United States during the 1990s?

3. According to the author, the heart of the abortion controversy is not about the fate of unborn babies. What does she believe the controversy is about?

Mandatory motherhood is a unique kind of slavery that specifically victimizes women and children. About one-third of the world's women live in countries where enforced motherhood rules the day. Not too long ago, perhaps women's biology was their destiny. But no more. With the advent of modern contraception and quality reproductive care, there's no excuse for forcing women to bear children against their will, or failing to provide basic maternal care, or compelling women to seek out illegal, unsafe abortions. There's no excuse for forcing children to be born unwanted, sentencing them to a probable life of dysfunction. The future of any society rests in its children, and a civilized society is one that invests in children and parents by providing a healthy, loving environment in which to raise kids.

Abortion is probably the world's most common surgical procedure. About 46 million abortions are performed every year, 20 million of them illegal. Abortion is practiced widely by women all over the world, across all social classes, and regardless of laws against abortion. Since the beginning of recorded history, abortion has been commonly practiced by almost all societies, including ancient China, Egypt, Greece, Rome, and countless others. In fact, abortion could be called a fundamental aspect of human behaviour.

But because abortion is still illegal or restricted in many countries today, two out of every five abortions in the world are performed unsafely—by an untrained provider or in an unclean setting. Every year, about 78,000 women die from unsafe and illegal abortions. For every death caused by unsafe abortion, several women are injured or left infertile. And countless unwanted children are born to women unable to obtain an abortion. Many of these kids will live a life marred by poverty, abuse, and neglect. . . .

Countries That Have Suffered Under Antiabortion Laws

Roughly one-third of the world's women live in countries with strict abortion legislation, where women are not allowed abortion under any circumstances, or only in cases of rape, incest, or where the woman's life or health is in danger. Here are some specific examples from a few countries where abortion is or was illegal.

Romania: Surviving Brutal Pro-Life Policies

In 1967, Romanian dictator Nicolai Ceausescu came to power and reversed that country's policy of legal and safe abortion. Although the birth rate initially increased, by the 1980s, it had shrunk back down to the mid-60s level because underground abortion networks had mushroomed. The drive to increase births was not accompanied by any basic medical or social improvements. Countless mothers and babies died for lack of medical care, food, and maternity beds. The country was so embarrassed at its soaring maternal and infant mortality rates that it abandoned international standards for recording them. Over the course of 20 years, an estimated 10,000 women died needlessly from illegal abortions alone. Ceausescu's action led to his downfall (he was executed in 1989), and it resulted in thousands of abandoned and neglected children whose plight moved the world.

One of the succeeding government's first acts was to legalize abortion as an emergency health measure. International family planning agencies were invited to set up clinics in Romania, and they found that 40% of women of childbearing age had reproductive tract damage left by illegal abortions. Continued economic chaos and lack of medical care means that Romania has a very high abortion rate even today, about 1.3 million for every half-million live births. Even so, almost 2,000 babies were abandoned at maternity hospitals in 1994. Countless thousands of children still languish today in orphanages, in squalid conditions, and another 10,000 wander the streets of Romanian cities, homeless. School enrollment has dropped by 21% since 1992 and over 400,000 children have quit school since 1992. About 2,500 Romanian kids are HIV positive, more than the combined total of all Western Europe. And dozens of pedophiles from Western Europe travel regularly to Romania because of its reputation as a country where children are desperate and vulnerable.

Given these deplorable conditions, it will probably take Romania several generations before it can hope to heal the human misery caused by Ceausescu's brutal policy against abortion and contraception. This country serves as a malignant example of the uncivilized consequences of so-called "pro-life" policies.

Latin America: The Crime of Unwanted Pregnancy

In Central and South America, abortion is illegal in every country except Cuba and Guyana, but it's widely practiced by all social classes. At least 4 million illegal abortions take place in Latin America every year, despite it being the most devoutly Roman Catholic region in the world. That's one of the highest documented rates of unsafe abortion in the world. In Brazil, about 1.5 million abortions occur every year, 250,000 women are hospitalized, and many thousands die. Perhaps you've heard of the serious epidemic of street kids in Rio de Janeiro, who are forced into crime and prostitution to support themselves. The police consider them vermin, sometimes shooting them like rats.

In Chile, one in three pregnant women choose to have an abortion—that's 160,000 a year—and hundreds die. Wealthy women in Chile (as in any country) can arrange a safe abortion in a hospital or private clinic for large sums of money. Poor women have to rely on unskilled practitioners, and when these women arrive in hospital emergency rooms with complications—37,000 women a year—they're often interrogated by medical staff and then reported to the police. Although only a handful of Chilean women are convicted and sent to jail, it's common for women to spend days or weeks in jail awaiting trial.

Africa: The High Incidence of Maternal Mortality

In Africa, very few countries allow abortion, and problems related to pregnancy are the leading cause of death for women of childbearing age, with complications from abortion consistently ranking at the top of the list. For every 100,000 abortions in Africa, 680 women die. That's over twice the average for developing nations, and about 680 times the number of developed countries. 58 women are known to die each day from trying to end their pregnancies with homemade cures or in unsafe underground clinics. Many public health experts say these figures likely represent a tiny tip of the iceberg.

In Ethiopia, 55 percent of maternal mortality stems from illegal abortion. In Nigeria, half of maternal deaths can be traced to this cause. Forty percent of the women who come to some public hospitals are there because of abortion complications and about a third of those die without leaving the hospital. . . .

Let's turn to a few countries that have more liberalized abortion policies. About two-thirds of the world's women live in countries with liberal or fairly liberal abortion laws, where women are allowed abortion to preserve their mental or physical health, or for social and economic reasons, or upon request without regard to reason.

The Netherlands: The Benefits of Sexual Education

In the Netherlands, abortion is freely available on demand. Yet the Netherlands boasts the lowest abortion rate in the world, about 6 abortions per 1,000 women per year, and the complication and death rates for abortion are miniscule. How do they do it? First of all, contraception is widely available and free—it's covered by the national health insurance plan. Holland also carries out extensive public education on contraception, family planning, and sexuality. An ethic of personal responsibility for one's sexual activity is strongly promoted. Of course, some people say that teaching kids about sex and contraception will only encourage them to have lots of sex. But Dutch teenagers tend to have less frequent sex, starting at an older age, than American teenagers, and the Dutch teenage pregnancy rate is 9 times lower than in the U.S.

An important message that we can learn from Holland and other European countries is that even the most comprehensive family planning programs and widespread contraceptive use will never completely eliminate the need for abortion. Abortion is a critical backstop to contraception, which is not 100% effective. And people do make mistakes—they sometimes forget to use their contraception, or they use it wrongly. Motherhood should never be a punishment for human error.

Sweden: Government Support for Parenting

In Sweden, abortion has been available upon request since 1973 until the 18th week of pregnancy, and sex education has been a compulsory subject in schools since 1956. At 19 abortions per 1,000 women per year, Sweden's abortion rate is three times higher than Holland's, and only 20% less than the rate of the United States, but the abortion rate for women under 25 is half that of the U.S.

Sweden is particularly interesting because its birth rate increased to more than two children per woman during the 1990s. The reason for the baby boom was the creation of a 15-month paid parental leave, a doubling of the number of day care centres, and other perks, such as paid leave for parents of sick children. The government's policy is not to increase the birth rate, though—it's to help children successfully integrate into society. A lesson can be learned from that policy, because many countries that made abortion illegal—Nazi Germany for instance—did it to increase the birth rate. Obviously, a far more humane and effective way of increasing the birth rate, as demonstrated by Sweden, is to give parents the time and the resources to raise children well.

Canada: Exercising Sensible Judgment

Canada has no law at all restricting abortion. The safety of abortion is governed just like any other medical procedure, and most abortions are funded by government health insurance. Because there's no law, antichoice groups in Canada complain about how women are having casual abortions right up to their ninth month of pregnancy, but in practice, 90% of abortions are performed in the first trimester, and no doctor will perform abortions past about 20 or 21 weeks unless it's for compelling health or genetic reasons. Just over 100,000 abortions are performed per year in Canada, a reasonably low rate of 16 per 1,000 women.

Canada also boasts what I believe is the lowest maternal mortality rate for early abortion in the entire world, 0.1 per 1,000 abortions. (In contrast, the Netherlands' rate is 0.2 per 1,000 abortions.) Canada serves as an excellent example of why any kind of legal restriction on abortion is completely unnecessary. Women exercise their sensible moral judgement and doctors exercise their professional medical judgement, and that's all that's needed to regulate the process.

The United States: Legal Gains Under Threat

America has had legal abortion on request since 1973. Before legalization, abortion complications accounted for 23% of all pregnancy-related admissions to municipal hospitals in New York City. After legalization, that number fell by 75% almost immediately, and continued to fall through the '70s and '80s. Today, the complication rate for early abortion in the United States is less than 1%, and the maternal mortality rate is 0.6 per 100,000 abortions.

However, the American woman's right to abortion and contraception has been undermined by extreme antichoice violence and harassment, and numerous legal, social, and political obstacles. America's large and politically powerful antichoice movement is also against contraception, with the result that 1.3 million American women still have abortions every year, a rate of 24 per 1,000 women, unnecessarily high for such an advanced, democratic country. The abortion rate has declined from a high of almost 1.6 million abortions in the early 1990s, due mostly to increased contraceptive use and reduced sexual activity amongst young people. However, America still has a very high rate of unintended and teenage pregnancies, and its mortality and complication rates from abortion, while low, could probably be improved.

Significantly, it's been shown that the presence of antiabortion protesters outside clinics actually increases the rate of abortion complications. A more tolerant attitude towards sexuality, contraception, and abortion would undoubtedly serve to reduce America's unplanned pregnancy and abortion rates, and further improve the safety of abortion. The experience of America shows that legal abortion makes a tremendous improvement to women's lives, but that an antichoice

The Core of the Women's Rights Issue

In a sane society that respected women and treated them as equals, abortion would not only be safe and legal—it would be fully funded and unrestricted. In order for women to be truly liberated, the material conditions must exist for women to live free from the burden of forced motherhood. That's why the right to abortion is at the core [of] any serious demand for women's rights.

Socialist Worker,
"Why Abortion Is Crucial To Women's Equality,"
May 11, 2007.

backlash can remove hard-won gains, resulting in more danger and less freedom for women.

When quality contraception is made available to people, and they use it properly, rates of unplanned pregnancy and abortion tend to go down significantly. In countries where abortion is legal, the differences in abortion rates can largely be attributed to effective contraceptive use. For example, in eastern Europe, where contraceptive use is very low, there are about 50–70 abortions per 1,000 women of childbearing age each year. By contrast, in western Europe where contraception is used widely, the average rate is 11 per 1,000 women. In general, the more widely available and accepted contraception is, and the more effective its use, the lower the rate of unintended pregnancy, and the lower the abortion rate. Of course, other factors affect the abortion rate, such as desired family size, economics, available social supports, and so on, but contraception probably contributes to larger reductions in abortion rates than all other factors combined....

The Plight of Unwanted Children

The antichoice suffer from what I call the "fetus focus fallacy." They put fetuses ahead of just about everything else, including women's lives and rights, the alleviation of human suffering, freedom of conscience and religion, and truth itself. But let's take a look at these "unborn children," the ones who end up being aborted, but who should, according to antiabortionists, be forced to live.

Unwanted childbearing has long been linked with adverse consequences to children. Several studies, conducted in countries like the U.S., Czechoslovakia, and Sweden, have documented the long-term developmental problems suffered by children whose mothers did not want to bear them. The findings point to various emotional, educational, and functional disorders that get worse as children become adults. These difficulties happen even to children born to healthy, adult women who have stable marriages and adequate economic resources. The problems are compounded for the majority of unwanted children who are born to poor, unhealthy, unmarried, or teenage mothers.

The studies focused on women who tried to get abortions and were denied them by law or by circumstance. Some used control groups of wanted children and compared them to groups of unwanted children. The studies found that when compared to wanted children, unwanted children are more likely to suffer from:

- crippling emotional handicaps
- stunted intellectual and educational development
- patterns of anti-social behaviour
- troubled home and family life
- abuse or neglect by parents
- dissatisfaction and dysfunction in adult life

For example, unwanted children are:

- significantly more likely to have mental handicaps at birth

- more likely to dislike school and perform significantly worse academically

- more than twice as likely to have a record of juvenile delinquency, up to four times more likely to have an adult criminal record, and three times more likely to be repeat offenders

- more likely to abuse alcohol and drugs in youth and early adulthood

- up to six times more likely to receive welfare between ages 16 and 21

- twice as likely to be less adaptive to frustration and stress, a handicap that continues into adulthood

- nearly three times more likely to describe themselves as unhappy and unable to cope with their problems

Family Planning Benefits Society

The findings of these studies of unwanted children paint a clear and disturbing picture of what happens to children when abortion and family planning services are restricted. Forced motherhood and a lack of social support mean that unplanned children too often become victims of life, simply through an accident of birth. And an unwanted child may become an unwanted adult. A recent study in the United States concluded that the legalization of abortion there in 1973 may account for half of the 30–40% reduction in crime that America has experienced since 1991. Legal abortion allows women and men to plan their families and provide for wanted children adequately. The result is more confident, happier, healthier children, who will be more likely to lead fulfilling and constructive lives than their unwanted counterparts.

Legal abortion benefits the health and well-being of children in other ways, too. Children are no longer orphaned when their mothers die from dangerous, illegal abortions, leaving their families without the critical economic and social contributions of a mother. And safe abortions enable women to bear wanted children later, instead of never because of infertility due to botched abortions.

Benefits of Legal Abortion

Besides the tremendous benefit to society of ensuring that every child is a wanted child, legal abortion has clearly been a significant factor in saving women's lives and health:

- A large majority of legal abortions replace abortions that had been performed illegally, and often unsafely, before the change in laws.

- Deaths from abortion have declined dramatically in all countries where abortion has been legalized. The risk of death from abortion has fallen steadily, and is now miniscule. The chances of dying in childbirth are now about 10 times greater.

- The chances of complications caused by childbirth are close to 30 times greater than complications caused by abortion. Abortion is nearly twice as safe as a penicillin injection.

- Where abortion is legal and readily available, women obtain abortions earlier in pregnancy when health risks to them are lowest.

- One-third of all legal abortions are on women for whom the health and social consequences of unplanned childbearing are the greatest—teenagers and women over 35.

- Legal abortion protects women suffering from serious or life-threatening illnesses and genetic disease that could be passed onto their children with devastating consequences.

- When women can control their reproduction, it leaves them free to pursue higher education and careers, and to plan their lives and families. Women should not be expected to sacrifice their personal and economic freedom to have babies they don't want.

Antiabortion Laws Denigrate Women

Despite the obvious health and social benefits, legal abortion continues to be the victim of profound, sometimes violent, controversy. The controversy is fueled by religious dogma, particularly that of the Catholic Church and fundamentalist religions, which claim that all life is sacred, and human life starts at conception. Even beyond religious doctrine, the social message is that choosing to continue a pregnancy is good; terminating it is bad, regardless of the circumstances. This attitude has a deep effect on women having abortions. Some women feel embarrassed, guilty, and ashamed for deciding to have an abortion. In fact, women who come to abortion clinics are often surprised when they receive professional, compassionate medical care. Abortion is probably the only medical service where the patient expects shabby treatment and an atmosphere of disapproval. That's because the well has been poisoned by years of antichoice propaganda, much of it inflammatory and grossly inaccurate. . . .

For the antichoice, I believe the heart of the abortion controversy is not about the fate of unborn babies. It's about the value of women in society. In North America, for example, many antiabortion leaders oppose ideas and programs that could help women achieve equality and freedom, and protect the health and well-being of families. For instance, they oppose affirmative action programs that help women gain equity

115

in the job market. They force poor women to have babies and then cut off their welfare. They lobby against health and nutrition programs for children. They condone the bombing of clinics providing reproductive services, and the killing of doctors and staff. These uncivilized actions reveal the true nature of antichoice goals. They want a return to the days when women had few choices in life. They don't like women having too much freedom, especially in controlling their reproductive lives. They're convinced that women can't be trusted to make their own decisions. And they certainly don't like women having sex for fun without paying for it.

Toward a Civilized World

The high rates of death and serious injury associated with unsafe and illegal abortion prove that governments, public health officials, and right-wing religious groups are blind and indifferent to the realities of women's lives. These people continue to believe that laws against abortion will stop abortion, in spite of obvious contrary evidence. The only thing that laws against abortion do is make abortion dangerous, turn most women into criminals, produce millions of disadvantaged children, and create wide disrespect for the law. When it's plain to see that tens of millions of women willingly *risk their lives* to end an unwanted pregnancy, the hypocrisy of those in power is nothing less than criminal. Much of the blame for this probably rests on the shoulders of more developed nations, who have failed to share enough of their wealth, technology, and experience with the rest of the world.

However, through the United Nations, the world has recently recognized the right of women everywhere to education and reproductive health care, the right to participate in the political process, and other important rights. In addition, there is an increasing amount of open discussion and concern about unsafe abortion within the international community. Efforts are being made in many countries to make abortion safer and more accessible even where it is illegal. These are very positive developments. But unfortunately, you won't find any United Nations document that asserts legal abortion as the right of all women everywhere. Safe abortion, yes. But not legal. It seems the world is not quite ready for that yet, even though I don't believe there can ever be such a thing as safe, *illegal* abortion.

We probably won't be able to change laws against abortion without some kind of universal consensus, like we have on slavery, but I believe we're getting closer and closer to that universal consensus. The day may soon come when women all around the world will have the legal right to decide for themselves when and whether to have children, and the means to exercise that right safely. And children will have the fundamental right to be wanted, to grow up safe, happy, and healthy. On that day, the world will become truly civilized.

| "About half of the drop in crime results from the Supreme Court's 1973 Roe v. Wade *decision legalizing abortion."*

Abortion Has Led to a Decrease in Crime

Robert Wanderer

In the following viewpoint, Robert Wanderer contends that the legalization of abortion in the United States has contributed to a decrease in crime. According to the author, statistics reveal that states that legalized abortion a few years before Roe v. Wade *witnessed drops in crime rates, and once the entire country legalized abortion, national statistics showed a similar trend. The reasoning behind all this, Wanderer states, is that unwanted children are more likely than wanted children to become criminals. Unwanted pregnancies are more likely to be aborted, and thus, fewer potential criminals are born. Robert Wanderer is a founding member of the San Francisco chapter of the International Society for General Semantics (ISGS) and a longtime editor of the chapter newsletter, the* Map. *He recently received the Talbot Winchell Award for furthering the understanding of general semantics.*

As you read, consider the following questions:

1. What age group accounts for the largest group of criminals?

2. How does the author prove, in his view, that a link exists between legalized abortion and falling crime rates?

3. Why is the theorized link between legalized abortion and crime highly controversial?

We learn as small children that if you put your hand on a hot stove, you're going to get burned. We learn a large number of these cause-and-effect relationships. And we understand more complex relationships: There are causes with more than one effect, and effects with more than one cause. Sometimes these relationships become extremely difficult to comprehend when the issue is more abstract.

Linking Legalized Abortion and Declining Crime Rates

For example, the crime rate in the United States: After remaining more or less constant for many years, the rate began declining sharply in the 1990s. What caused this? Police, law enforcement officials, and politicians all claimed credit, but their actions do not explain the large, widespread, and persistent drop in crime.

Two researchers, John J. Donohue III of the Stanford Law School and Steven D. Levitt of the University of Chicago, have advanced a startling and provocative theory, supported by substantial evidence: About half of the drop in crime results from the Supreme Court's 1973 *Roe v. Wade* decision legalizing abortion.

Their reasoning goes:

* The largest group of criminals is between ages 18 and 24. The sharp decline in crime began 18 years after abortion

---

The Newspapers' Explanations

Crime-Drop Explanation	Number of Citations
1. Innovative policing strategies	52
2. Increased reliance or prisons	47
3. Changes in crack and other drug markets	33
4. Aging of the population	32
5. Tougher gun-control laws	32
6. Strong economy	28
7. Increased number of police	26
8. All other explanations (increased use of capital punishment, concealed-weapons laws, gun buybacks, and others)	34

TAKEN FROM: Steven D. Levitt and Stephen J. Dubner, *Freakonomics*, 2006.

---

became legal and the number of abortions shot up from under 750,000 in 1973 to 1.6 million by 1980.

* Five states which legalized abortion a few years before the Supreme Court decision noted a drop in crime a few years earlier than other states.

* Even allowing for other factors, states with a high rate of abortion have experienced a greater reduction in crime since 1985.

* Declines in crime are concentrated among men under 25 in the high-abortion states. The decrease is not so much a matter of fewer men in that age group as less crime per capita.

* Unwanted children are more likely than wanted children to become criminals. Unwanted pregnancies are more likely to be aborted.

* Legal abortion provides women an opportunity to control childbearing. If a woman who has had several children says "enough," she can do this when abortion is legal and available.

* Women who choose to have abortions are not a random sample of all women: They are inclined to be teenagers, unmarried and/or minority people in which groups the possibility of sons turning to crime is greater than in the general population.

Controversy Surrounding the Abortion/Crime Link

All in all, the study's authors estimate that legal abortions account for about half of the decline in crime in the 1990s. They predict a continuing, although slower, decline in crime over the next twenty years.

This statistic-packed and rigorously-argued paper has been termed "striking" and "persuasive" by judges and legal experts who have reviewed it.

What, then, is likely to happen as a result of this study? The chief problem here is that people tend to believe what they want to believe. People who regard abortion as immoral might dismiss this thesis out of hand. Even those who accept a woman's right to choose may be uncomfortable with the subject. The authors cite the experience of the former police chief of Minneapolis who wrote in 1990 that "abortion is the only effective crime prevention device since the 1960s." When he ran for governor four years later, his opinion was given publicity, and his poll figures promptly plummeted.

An interesting test of your openness to new ideas: If you accept the researchers' well-presented thesis, do you think it should be used to support policies by government and/or public service groups urging voluntary abortions of selected pregnancies?

> *"Even if abortion did lower crime by culling out 'unwanted' children, this effect would be greatly outweighed by the rise in crime associated with the greater incidence of single-parent families that also follows from abortion liberalization."*

Abortion Has Not Led to a Decrease in Crime

John R. Lott, Jr.

In the following viewpoint, John R. Lott, Jr., a research scientist at the University of Maryland, rejects notions that abortion has decreased crime supposedly because it has kept numerous disadvantaged youths from being born into lives of poverty and crime. Lott maintains that the ease of obtaining an abortion prompted many people to engage in more unprotected sex and led to a rise in out-of-wedlock births. Because out-of-wedlock children are more likely to commit crime, according to Lott, it is statistically correct to conclude that the passing of pro-abortion laws has led to an increase in crime.

John R. Lott, Jr., "Abortion and Crime: One Has an Effect on the Other, but It May Not Be the Effect You Think," *National Review*, vol. 59, August 13, 2007, pp. 18–22. Copyright © 2007 by National Review, Inc., 215 Lexington Avenue, New York, NY 10016. Reproduced by permission.

As you read, consider the following questions:

1. What flaw does John R. Lott Jr. see in the 1966 study by Hans Forssman and Inga Thuwe?

2. According to Lott, by what percentage did out-of-wedlock births increase between 1985 and 1989?

3. Why does Lott believe it is important to examine Canadian statistics when debating the "abortion decreases crime" theory?

Violent crime in the United States shot up like a rocket after 1960. From 1960 to 1991, reported violent crime increased by an incredible 372 percent. This disturbing trend was seen across the country, with robbery peaking in 1991 and rape and aggravated assault following in 1992. But then something unexpected happened: Between 1991 and 2000, rates of violent crime and property crime fell sharply, dropping by 33 percent and 30 percent, respectively. Murder rates were stable up to 1991, but then plunged by a steep 44 percent.

Several plausible explanations have been advanced for the drop during the 1990s. Some stress law-enforcement measures, such as higher arrest and conviction rates, longer prison sentences, "broken windows" police strategies, and the death penalty. Others emphasize right-to-carry laws for concealed handguns, a strong economy, or the waning of the crack-cocaine epidemic.

Of all the explanations, perhaps the most controversial is the one that attributes lower crime rates in the '90s to *Roe v. Wade*, the Supreme Court's 1973 decision to mandate legalized abortion. According to this argument, the large number of women who began having abortions shortly after *Roe* were most likely unmarried, in their teens, or poor, and their children would have been "unwanted." Children born in these circumstances would have had a higher-than-average likelihood of becoming criminals, and would have entered their teens—their "criminal prime"—in the early 1990s. But because they were aborted, they were not around to make trouble.

This is an attention-grabbing theory, to be sure. But a thorough analysis of abortion and crime statistics leads to the opposite conclusion: that abortion increases crime.

Looking for a Correlation

Debate about the relationship between abortion and crime was greatly influenced by a Swedish study published in 1966 by Hans Forssman and Inga Thuwe. They followed the children of 188 women who were denied abortions from 1939 to 1941 at the only hospital in Gothenburg [Göteburg], Sweden. Their study compared these "unwanted" children with another group, this one composed of the first child born at the hospital after each of the "unwanted" children. They found that the "unwanted" children were much more likely to grow up in adverse conditions—for example, with divorced parents, or in foster homes. These children were also more likely to become delinquents and have trouble in school. Unfortunately, the authors never investigated whether the children's "unwantedness" caused their problems, or were simply correlated with them.

Forssman and Thuwe's claim, notwithstanding the limits of the data supporting it, became axiomatic among supporters of legalized abortion. During the 1960s and '70s, before *Roe*, abortion rights advocates attributed all sorts of social ills, including crime and mental illness, to "unwanted" children. Weeding these poor, crime-prone people out of the population through abortion was presented as a way to make society safer.

Recently, John Donohue and Steven Levitt—a law professor and an economist, respectively—revived the debate. They presented evidence that supposedly demonstrated abortion's staggeringly large effect on crime rates, and argued that up to

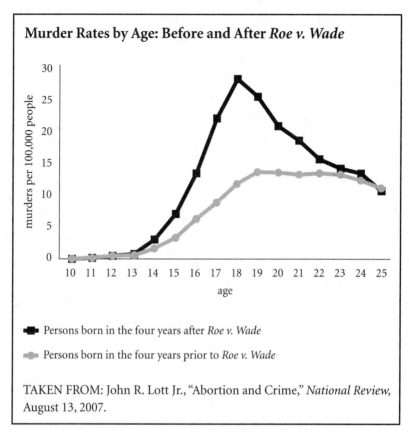

Murder Rates by Age: Before and After *Roe v. Wade*

■ Persons born in the four years after *Roe v. Wade*

● Persons born in the four years prior to *Roe v. Wade*

TAKEN FROM: John R. Lott Jr., "Abortion and Crime," *National Review,* August 13, 2007.

"one-half of the overall crime reduction" between 1991 and 1997, and up to 81 percent of the drop in murder rates during that period, was attributable to the rise in abortions in the early to mid 1970s. If that claim was accurate, they had surely found the Holy Grail of crime reduction.

Most people who challenge the "abortion reduces crime" argument do so on ethical grounds, rather than trying to rebut the empirical evidence. But it is worth looking at the data, too—because they do not prove what they are supposed to.

The Rise of Single-Parent Families

To understand why abortion might not cut crime, one should first consider how dramatically it changed sexual relationships. Once abortion became widely available, people engaged in much more premarital sex, and also took less care in using contraceptives. Abortion, after all, offered a backup if a woman got pregnant, making premarital sex, and the nonuse of contraception, less risky. In practice, however, many women found that they couldn't go through with an abortion, and out-of-wedlock births soared. Few of these children born out of wedlock were put up for adoption; most women who were unwilling to have abortions were also unwilling to give up their children. Abortion also eliminated the social pressure on men to marry women who got pregnant. All of these outcomes—more out-of-wedlock births, fewer adoptions than expected, and less pressure on men "to do the right thing"—led to a sharp increase in single-parent families.

Multiple studies document this change. From the early 1970s through the late 1980s, as abortion became more and more frequent, there was a tremendous increase in the rate of out-of-wedlock births, from an average of 5 percent (1965–69) to over 16 percent twenty years later (1985–89). Among blacks, the number jumped from 35 percent to 62 percent. While not all of this rise can be attributed to liberalized abortion laws, they were certainly a key contributor.

What happened to all these children raised by single women? No matter how much they want their children, single parents tend to devote less attention to them than married couples do. Single parents are less likely than married parents to read to their children or take them on excursions, and more likely to feel angry at their children or to feel that they are burdensome. Children raised out of wedlock have more social and developmental problems than children of married couples by almost any measure—from grades to school expulsion to disease. Unsurprisingly, children from unmarried families are also more likely to become criminals.

So the opposing lines of argument in the "abortion reduces crime" debate are clear: One side stresses that abortion eliminates "unwanted" children, the other that it increases out-of-wedlock births. The question is: Which consequence of abortion has the bigger impact on crime?

The Statistics Reveal the Truth

Unfortunately for those who argue that abortion reduces crime, Donohue and Levitt's research suffered from methodological flaws. As the *Economist* noted, "Donohue and Levitt did not run the test they thought they had." Work by two economists at the Boston Federal Reserve [Federal Reserve Bank of Boston], Christopher Foote and Christopher Goetz, found that, when the test was run correctly, it indicated that abortion actually *increases* violent crime. John Whitley and I had written an earlier study that found a similar connection between abortion and murder—namely, that legalizing abortion raised the murder rate, on average, by about 7 percent.

The "abortion decreases crime" theory runs into even more problems when the population is analyzed by age group. Suppose that liberalizing abortion in the early 1970s can indeed explain up to 80 percent of the drop in murder during the 1990s, as Donohue and Levitt claim. Deregulating abortion would then reduce criminality first among age groups born after the abortion laws changed, when the "unwanted," crime-prone elements began to be weeded out. Yet when we look at the declining murder rate during the 1990s, we find that this is not the case at all. Instead, murder rates began falling first among an older generation—those over 26—born before *Roe*. It was only later that criminality among those born after *Roe* began to decline.

Legalizing abortion increased crime. Those born in the four years after *Roe* were much more likely to commit murder than those born in the four years prior. This was especially true when they were in their "criminal prime . . ."

The "abortion decreases crime" argument gets even weaker when we look at data from Canada. While crime rates in both the United States and Canada began declining at the same time, Canada liberalized its abortion laws much later than the U.S. did. Although Quebec effectively legalized abortion in late 1976, it wasn't until 1988, in a case originating in Ontario, that the Canadian Supreme Court struck down limits on abortion nationwide. If the legalization of abortion in the U.S. caused crime to begin dropping 18 years later, why did the crime rate begin falling just three years after the comparable legal change in Canada?

Even if abortion did lower crime by culling out "unwanted" children, this effect would be greatly outweighed by the rise in crime associated with the greater incidence of single-parent families that also follows from abortion liberalization. In short, more abortions have brought more crime.

Periodical Bibliography

The following articles have been selected to supplement the diverse views presented in this chapter.

Joyce Arthur	"No, Virginia, Abortion Is NOT Genocide," *Humanist*, July-August 2000.
Mitchell B. Chamlin et al.	"Abortion as Crime Control: A Cautionary Tale," *Criminal Justice Policy Review*, June 2008.
Michele Kort	"Are U.S. Policies Killing Women?" *Ms.*, Winter 2008.
Sheryl McCarthy	"Behind the Abortion Color Line," *Nation*, April 27, 2009.
William McGurn	"The NAACP and Black Abortions," *Wall Street Journal*, July 15, 2008.
D.W. Miller	"Exploring the Link Between Abortion and Crime Rates," *Chronicle of Higher Education*, May 18, 2001.
Randall K. O'Bannon	"Abortion No Stimulus for Economy," *National Right to Life*, February 2009.
Jacob Weisberg	"What Happened to Family Values?" *Newsweek*, September 15, 2008.

CHAPTER 4

Is Abortion Safe?

Chapter Preface

The U.S. Food and Drug Administration (FDA) approved Plan B, an emergency contraception pill, for use in 1999, but it required a doctor's prescription. After years of delay, the FDA decided in 2006 that Plan B could be sold over the counter—but only to women eighteen and older. Girls seventeen and under still needed a doctor's prescription.

Under President Barack Obama's administration, the FDA has amended its previous decision and will allow seventeen-year-olds to purchase the morning-after pill without a prescription by 2010, and it is possible that all age restrictions on the drug will be removed.

Plan B is not the same as RU-486. Both are called "morning-after pills," which is confusing, but RU-486 also carries the label "abortion pill." RU-486 works by causing a woman's body to abort a fetus within the first two months of a pregnancy. Plan B, on the other hand, works by preventing ovulation and fertilization, and does not allow an egg to implant after intercourse. Plan B must be taken within three days of unprotected sex and is ineffective if the woman is already pregnant.

Since the net result is to prevent pregnancy from happening, pro-choice groups welcome the loosening of restrictions on Plan B sales. They claim that Plan B protects the health of young women. As Planned Parenthood puts it, "This decision is commonsense policy that will help reduce the number of unintended pregnancies and protect the health and safety of all women."

Pro-life groups disagree, and use the same issue—women's health—to criticize Plan B. Their experts warn that if Plan B is readily available, teenagers will simply indulge in more unprotected sex. In fact, they point to a few cases in which teenage girls were given free packages of Plan B, but failed to use the pills. In addition, they warn that the Plan B pill contains the hormone levonorgestrel, found in many birth control pills. That hormone can increase a woman's risk of getting blood clots or experiencing a heart attack or stroke. The conservative Christian organization Concerned Women for America says, "Plan B is a high dose of birth control pills. . . . The FDA violated its standards when it made the high-dose Plan B available nonprescription to adults. But now the FDA is making the drug available to minors without parental consent. . . . Parents should be furious that the FDA is putting their minor daughters at risk."

The following chapter presents arguments taken from non-profit organizations, religious organizations, and expert testimony before Congress. Like the Plan B debate, these arguments focus on abortion and women's health. Both sides in the debate cite valid concerns about the long- and short-term effects of abortion procedures on a woman's emotional and physical well-being, and each pledges that its views put women's health first.

> *"The Abortion Breast Cancer Link is not likely to be disproved because this finding rests on the biological facts about our created bodies."*

Abortion Increases the Risk for Breast Cancer

Angela Lanfranchi

In the viewpoint that follows, Angela Lanfranchi catalogs and analyzes the evidence showing a link between women experiencing abortion and an increase in their risk for developing breast cancer. Lanfranchi argues that this link exists, and has been proven time and again by scientific evidence that is largely ignored by the scientific community and the public. She contends that studies denying this link are filled with errors and that a larger movement in the scientific and medical communities has worked to suppress the evidence of a link. Lanfranchi is a practicing surgeon who specializes in breast cancer treatment. She also co-founded and serves as vice president of the Breast Cancer Prevention Institute.

Angela Lanfranchi, "Abortion and Breast Cancer: The Link That Won't Go Away," United States Conference of Catholic Bishops, June 28, 2007. Reproduced by permission.

As you read, consider the following questions:

1. The author reports that incidences of breast cancer have risen with legal abortion in what countries?

2. According to Angela Lanfranchi, how does carrying a pregnancy to full term protect a woman from breast cancer?

3. What errors does the author identify in studies denying the link between breast cancer and abortion?

There are many well-established and well-known causes of breast cancer, such as inheriting a BRCA gene (a defective gene associated with increased breast cancer risk) and being exposed to oral contraceptives and hormone replacement therapy. There are lesser known risks of breast cancer such as cigarette smoking before a full-term pregnancy and induced abortion. But just as only 15% of people who smoke will get lung cancer and only about 5–10% of women with breast cancer develop this cancer because they had an abortion, we should still advise the public of these avoidable risks, however small. The vast majority of women with breast cancer have not had an abortion, but there are some women with breast cancer that have abortion as an attributable risk. Women need this information to make informed choices and to understand when to get screened for cancer if they are at increased risk, beginning approximately 8 to 10 years after the risk was taken.

A Well-Documented Link

Over fifty years ago, in April 1957, the first study reporting a link between abortion and an increased risk of breast cancer was published in a major medical journal. At a time when few countries had legalized abortion, the authors found that Japanese women who'd had an abortion had nearly three times as high a risk of breast cancer as those who had not. By 1995, after abortion was widely legalized in the West, 17 studies worldwide (8 of them studying American women) showed a statistically significant abortion-breast cancer link (or "ABC link"). Yet few medical professionals or members of the public knew of these important studies.

Over the last thirty years, 48 million abortions have been done on American women and breast cancer incidence has risen 40%. The pattern has been seen in other countries as well. Romania enjoyed one of the lowest breast cancer rates when abortion was illegal, but has developed one of the world's highest rates since abortion was legalized. In the United Kingdom, breast cancer rates parallel abortion rates, with highest rates in England and lowest in Northern Ireland. China has had a 40% increase in breast cancer rates since it implemented its policy of one-child-per-family and forced abortions. Actuary Patrick Carroll, looking at data from several countries, concluded that abortion is the greatest predictor of a country's breast cancer rate.

Denial in the Scientific Community

Over ten years ago, in 1996, Dr. Joel Brind and colleagues from Pennsylvania State University published a meta-analysis of all the known published studies to date on breast cancer that distinguished between induced and spontaneous abortions (miscarriages). That rigorous quantitative analysis demonstrated a 30% increased risk of breast cancer in women who had an induced abortion. It established induced abortion as an independent risk for breast cancer, beyond the indisputable fact that women who abort lose the naturally occurring protection against breast cancer that develops by carrying the pregnancy to full term. The publication of these findings created a furor among those who believed this information would adversely affect reproductive "choice." Dr. Stuart Donnan, editor of the British journal where it was published, commented that some critics were trying to practice an "excessive paternalistic censorship . . . of the data" on the ABC link.

In the United States, Dr. Janet Daling also sparked controversy when she published her findings in the *Journal of the National Cancer Institute* (JNCI) in 1994. Daling's study showed a statistically significant increased risk of breast cancer in women with induced abortion, especially young women with a family history of cancer. But an accompanying editorial downplayed the results, saying that "it is difficult to see how they will be informative to the public." Dr. Daling responded to critics that she was adamantly pro-choice, had three sisters with breast cancer, and wished the results of her study had been different, but her data were "rock solid." When asked to speak on the topic, she declined, saying she "was tired of having rocks thrown at her."

In the last ten years, many studies have been published claiming there is no ABC link. Dr. Brind published an analysis of those studies in 2005, demonstrating flaws in their design, methods and statistical analysis. To understand these flaws, it is useful to review the biology that underlies and explains the ABC link, and the reasons why some may want to deny this inconvenient truth.

Pregnancy Protects Against Breast Cancer

In the 1970s, when researcher Dr. Irma Russo purchased some rats for breast cancer research, the dealer assured her they would reliably form breast cancers when given a carcinogen— provided she kept them from becoming pregnant first. She decided to investigate why a carcinogen would not cause cancer in rats with a litter of pups. In 1980, Drs. Jose and Irma Russo published their findings: About 70% of both aborted and virgin rats developed breast cancer when exposed to a carcinogen, but rats that had given birth before exposure were protected from cancer.

Years of published research have shed light on the breast maturation process that accounts for the protective effect of a full-term pregnancy. During pregnancy breasts enlarge, doubling in volume. Due to the stimulating hormones estrogen and progesterone, the number of lobules (units of breast tissue comprised of a duct and several milk glands) increases in preparation for breast feeding. Under the influence of the pheromones hCG and hPL, made by a baby in his mother's womb, the mother's breast also matures so that cancer-vulnerable Type 1 and 2 lobules become cancer resistant Type 4 lobules containing milk. Type 4 lobules later regress to Type 3 after weaning, but retain the genetic changes which make them cancer resistant.

Most of the breast maturation needed for resistance to breast cancer does not occur, however, until after 32 weeks of pregnancy, and gaining maximum protection at 40 weeks (full term). This is why a premature delivery before 32 weeks more than doubles breast cancer risk. Induced abortion before 32 weeks also increases the risk, in proportion to the length of pregnancy before the abortion occurs. A pregnancy ending between 32 and 36 weeks has about 90% of the protective effect of a full-term pregnancy of 40 weeks. In terms of breast cancer risk, there is no difference between a premature delivery and a late-term abortion before 32 weeks because the hormonal changes to the breast are the same and they differ only in whether or not the baby is alive when the pregnancy ends.

Distinguishing the Effects of Miscarriage from Abortion

About 23% of all pregnancies end in spontaneous abortions (i.e., miscarriages) in the first 11 weeks (in the first trimester). In most first-trimester pregnancies which end in miscarriage, the pregnancy hormones are lower than in a normal pregnancy due to either fetal or ovarian abnormality. (This is why women who miscarry at this stage may report never having felt pregnant.) Therefore, the breasts may not grow a significant number of Type 1 and 2 lobules (the places where cancer starts) in response to the pregnancy. Early miscarriage therefore does not increase the risk of breast cancer as does an induced abortion terminating a normal pregnancy.

A woman who is pregnant can legally choose an abortion or carry her baby to full term. By carrying her baby to full term, she matures about 85% of her breast tissue to cancer-resistant lobules, thereby lowering her long-term breast cancer risk, just by that fact alone. She loses the protective effect through abortion.

The "independent risk," i.e., leaving her breasts with more places for cancer to start, is contested by some epidemiologic studies, but is consistent with all known facts of breast development in texts and literature. She has permanent changes in her breasts caused by the pregnancy hormones and the baby's pheromones. These changes will *not* reduce cancer risk unless the pregnancy continues to at least 32 weeks. If pregnancy is interrupted, her breasts are left with more cancer-susceptible lobules than when her pregnancy began.

Additionally, forty-nine studies have concluded that induced abortion increases the risk of premature delivery in a subsequent pregnancy. So induced abortion not only adversely affects the health of later children who may be born prematurely, but it can also increase the mother's health risk of developing breast cancer.

Errors in Studies Denying the Link

Studies in the last ten years showing little or no association between breast cancer and abortion have so many flaws that they prompted Dr. Edward Furton, staff ethicist at the National Catholic Bioethics Center, to write "The Corruption of Science by Ideology" in 2004. Dr. Furton decried the "unwillingness of scientists to speak out against the shoddy research that is being advanced by those who deny the abortion-breast cancer link."

For example, in 2004 the British journal *Lancet* published a meta-analysis by Valerie Beral et al. of 52 abortion-breast

Courts Require Abortion Clinics to Inform Patients of Risks

Despite the worst efforts of scientists, doctors, politicians, journalists, and judges to quash public knowledge of the ABC [abortion-breast cancer] link, the fact that published evidence of it abounds would make it a daunting task to convince a jury of its nonexistence, given a well-presented case. Along these lines, two recent medical malpractice cases give cause for optimism. Both were filed by young women against abortion providers for failure to warn about the risk of breast cancer and psychological complications. Both were filed in reference to abortions that were obtained when the women were minors, and were filed in politically liberal jurisdictions. Importantly, both were also filed by women who did not have breast cancer. The first [*Stephanie Carter v. Charles E. Benjamin and Cherry Hill Women's Center*], in Philadelphia, Pennsylvania, was settled late in 2003 for an undisclosed but substantial amount, when the case was on the brink of jury selection. The second [a lawsuit against the All Women's Health Service Clinic located in Portland] was adjudicated in January 2005 in Portland, Oregon. Importantly, this was not a settlement, but rather was a judgment of liability following the entry of the equivalent of a plea of no contest by the abortion clinic. It also involved an undisclosed but substantial cash award to the plaintiff. All indications are that this is only the beginning of what may become a legal avalanche.

Joel Brind, "The Abortion-Breast Cancer Connection,"
National Catholic Bioethics Quarterly, *Summer 2005*.

cancer studies. In a meta-analysis, data is reanalyzed from existing studies to show an overall trend. Results can be skewed by including studies not based on sound scientific methodology, and by ignoring studies that contradict the researchers' desired outcome. Inexplicably, data from more than half the studies selected by Beral (28 of 52) had not even been published in peer-reviewed journals. Beral also excluded 15 peer-reviewed studies—whose findings supported the ABC link—for invalid, non-scientific reasons (e.g., the principal investigator could not be found, perhaps due to his death or retirement in the intervening 20 years). Ten of the 15 excluded studies showed a statistically significant association between abortion and breast cancer; collectively the excluded studies showed about an 80% increased risk after abortion. Furthermore, Beral *included* three studies known to have major methodological flaws, including one that misclassified 60,000 women as not having had abortions when government records show they did.

Another error in the Beral study, common to studies finding no ABC link, is to discount data from retrospective studies on the ground of "recall bias." The assumption is that women with breast cancer when interviewed about abortion history will more accurately recall and report their past abortions than those without breast cancer. Recall bias has been studied several times, and found to be nonexistent.

A third error made by Beral and others is to use an inappropriate comparison group. For example, they compare women who aborted a pregnancy to women who have never been pregnant. But the more valid comparison is to pregnant women who carried to term. As soon as a woman becomes pregnant (even before implantation), her estrogen levels start to rise, causing the number of Type 1 and 2 lobules to increase. Thereafter she is physiologically different from a woman who has never been pregnant. Two studies published in 1999 showed that breast cancer risk more than doubled when pregnancy ended before 32 weeks from induced abortion, late miscarriage or premature birth.

A study by Karin Michels et al., published in the April 2007 *Archives of Internal Medicine,* was reported in the *New York Times* and other news outlets as showing "Breast Cancer Not Linked to Abortion." This study began with over 100,000 women between 29 and 46 years of age, and interviewed them every two years about abortions, miscarriages and new breast cancer diagnoses. In finding no statistically significant association between abortion and breast cancer, the researchers committed at least 5 serious errors which have recently been detailed in the medical literature. Particularly egregious was the deletion of an important adjustment for spontaneous abortions from the overall result. This flaw alone reduced the reported risk increase from an almost significant 10% to a nonsignificant 1%. Also striking was the authors' complete omission of mention of the only other primary research study on the ABC link which Michels herself had co-authored. This was a 1995 study of Greek women, which had reported a statistically significant 51% increase in breast cancer risk with abortion, an increase that was specifically claimed not to have resulted from "recall bias." But in her latest study, Michels still relied on the discredited recall bias hypothesis, and mention of her earlier study would have contradicted that claim.

Scientific Bias Against the ABC Link

First, while we may idealize scientists as being above all personal biases and influences, the reality is that they, too, are human and can be influenced by many things other than the facts. Those influences may include cultural prejudices, sources of funding for research, and even sheer resistance to new or unwelcome ideas.

In a 2005 study "Scientists Behaving Badly," the scientific journal *Nature* revealed that, in an anonymous questionnaire, 15.5% of scientists who received grants from the National Institutes of Health admitted to changing study design, results and methodologies "in response to pressure from a funding source." Scientists studying cancer depend largely on grants from the National Cancer Institute [NCI]—and the NCI has shown a definite bias on this issue, inviting no known defender of the ABC link to present on this issue at its 2003 workshop convened ostensibly to discuss such questions.

Resistance to information whose source is considered "out of the mainstream" is common enough in scientific circles to have its own name, the Semmelweis Phenomenon. In the 1840s, before the germ theory of disease was widely accepted, Dr. Ignaz Semmelweis proved that hand-washing saved women's lives in maternity wards, reducing mortality to 3% from 30%. Yet the medical establishment ignored his findings for decades.

The Link Is Here to Stay

This tendency to ignore or deny inconvenient information is especially strong when the subject is abortion. Documentation and public awareness of the negative effects of abortion— especially the ABC link, and emotional and psychological difficulties after abortion—poses a danger to Big Abortion, in the same way studies linking cigarettes to cancer posed a danger to Big Tobacco.

The first study linking cigarettes to lung cancer was published in 1928, and the first surgeon general's warning, without the support of the AMA [American Medical Association], was announced in 1964. The Bradford-Hill epidemiologic criteria developed to evaluate causality, ultimately used to show the tobacco-lung cancer link in the 1960s, are the same criteria that support the ABC link.

The Abortion Breast Cancer Link is not likely to be disproved, because this finding rests on the biological facts about our created bodies. Pro-choice columnist Ellen Goodman in 2004 railed that research linking breast cancer to abortion "keeps reappearing no matter how many scientists drive a stake through its heart." But the link is based on how we are made, and this reality won't ever go away.

> *"Women seeking abortions in Mississippi must first sign a form indicating they've been told abortion can increase their risk of breast cancer. They aren't told that scientific reviews have concluded there is no such risk."*

Abortion Does Not Increase the Risk for Breast Cancer

Women's Health Weekly

The following viewpoint claims that the purported link between breast cancer and abortion by antichoice activists is false and based on unsubstantiated evidence. Even though the National Cancer Institute concluded that no suck link between breast cancer and abortion exists, antiabortion activists continue to push the idea. In some states, women must receive false information about how abortion causes breast cancer before they can have an abortion. The viewpoint concludes that publicizing the false link is just one more tactic employed by the pro-life campaign to frighten women and society into pro-life support. Newsrx.com publishes the largest weekly database of current medical news, disease research, and business reports for the pharmaceutical and biotech industries, updating its online database with thousands of articles each week.

As you read, consider the following questions:

1. What form must women seeking abortions in the state of Mississippi sign?

2. What did the studies conducted by the National Cancer Institute conclude about the link between abortion and breast cancer?

3. Why does Joel Brind, a biochemist at Baruch College in New York, believe that a link between abortion and breast cancer exists?

Women seeking abortions in Mississippi must first sign a form indicating they've been told abortion can increase their risk of breast cancer. They aren't told that scientific reviews have concluded there is no such risk.

Similar information suggesting a cancer link is given to women considering abortion in Texas, Louisiana and Kansas, and legislation to require such notification has been introduced in 14 other states.

Abortion opponents, who are pushing these measures, say they are simply giving women information to consider. But abortion rights supporters see it much differently.

"In my experience, this inaccurate information is going to dissuade few women from going ahead and having the abortion," said Vanessa Cullins, MD, vice president for medical affairs at Planned Parenthood Federation of America. "What it does do is put a false guilt trip and fear trip on that woman."

The Purported Abortion/Breast Cancer Link

More than a year ago, a panel of scientists convened by the National Cancer Institute (NCI) reviewed available data and concluded there is no link. A scientific review in the *Lancet*, a British medical journal, came to the same conclusion, questioning the methodology in a few studies that have suggested a link.

Still, information suggesting a link is being given to women to read during mandatory waiting periods before abortions. In some cases, the information is on the states' Web sites.

"We're going to continue to educate the public about this," said Karen Malec, president of the Coalition on Abortion/ Breast Cancer, an antiabortion group. The effort to write the issue into state law began in the mid-1990s, when a few studies suggested women who had abortions or miscarriages might be more likely to develop breast cancer. The warnings are now required in Texas and Mississippi, and health officials in Kansas and Louisiana issue them voluntarily.

Minnesota law requires its health department to include this information on its Web site, but the department backed down after an outcry from the state's medical community. Montana law also mandated the warning, but the state Supreme Court struck it down.

The brochures still in circulation tell women the issue "needs further study."

"They can do further research on their own and determine which of those studies they should put most attention on," said Sharon Watson, spokeswoman for the Kansas Department of Health and Environment. "We're just trying to provide all the information it's possible to provide."

Changing Policies

Louisiana, which elected a Democratic governor last year, replacing a Republican—is going to change its official literature that mentions the cancer link, said Bob Johannessen, spokesman for the state's Department of Health and Hospitals. He said the department's new director did not know the state pamphlet included such information until contacted this week by the Associated Press.

Culture and Acceptance of Abortion

The need to make sense of an experience like having an abortion, replete with moral and cultural attachments, is not surprising. Researchers have tied self-esteem to the belief that people are consistent with shared cultural values.... In American culture there is a recurring public dialogue on abortion that occurs at least each election cycle. Also public demonstrations both in favour of and against abortion are not uncommon. Contact with anti-abortion sentiments or protesters may influence women's opinion that by having an abortion one is not living up to others' cultural values. Abortion as a source of political mobilization has been explored. Making sense of the experience of abortion leads women.... to work on reproductive issues. Culture therefore can shape the nature of women's sense making, not only by influencing their involvement in a public discourse on abortion, but with private practices such as using rituals to make sense of personal abortion experiences.

JoAnn Trybulski,
"Making Sense: Women's Abortion Experiences,"
British Journal of Midwifery, *vol. 16, no. 9,*
September 2008.

"If there is scientific evidence, and it certainly appears there now is, we would certainly make the necessary changes in that brochure," he said November 9, 2004. The brochure, he said, is a reflection of the "very, very strong pro-family, pro-life leaning" of Louisiana.

"Nonetheless, it's incumbent on us as the health agency to make sure any information is factually correct," he said. "We don't want to be misleading women who are making this important choice."

The issue continues to be debated in state legislatures, with bills considered this year in Georgia, Hawaii, Illinois, Iowa, Massachusetts, Minnesota, New Hampshire, New Jersey, New York, North Carolina, Oklahoma, Vermont, Washington and West Virginia.

On the federal level, several members of Congress complained last year after the NCI Web site included material suggesting a link between breast cancer and abortion or miscarriage. An expert panel that was asked to review the data reported in March 2003 that "well established" evidence shows no link.

Among the studies cited by the NCI expert panel was Danish research that used computerized medical records to compare women who had undergone abortions with that country's cancer registry and found no higher cancer rate.

"The virtually complete consensus was that the studies that purported to show a link were methodologically flawed," said Dr. Martin Abeloff, director of the [Sidney] Kimmel Comprehensive Cancer Center at Johns Hopkins University. Those studies that showed no link, he said, were almost all well done.

The Debate Continues

Still, antiabortion activists are unconvinced.

Joel Brind, a biochemist at Baruch College in New York who advises the Coalition on Abortion/Breast Cancer, noted that a woman's chances of getting breast cancer go down if she gives birth at a relatively young age. He reasons that those who opt for abortion are giving up a chance of reducing their breast cancer risk.

Therefore, he says, abortion increases the risk of cancer.

He participated in the NCI debate—filing a minority report—and dismisses the panel's findings. "It was basically a political exercise," he said, "a charade if you will."

| "In approving RU-486, the FDA showed
  that science and good sense can still
  carry the day, even in an election year."

RU-486 Is Safe

The Nation

*RU-486, a synthetic steroid compound (also known as
mifepristone) used in abortion pills, has been labeled unsafe by
the pro-life movement, prompting government review of the
drug's approval and use. In the viewpoint that follows, The Nation writes that charges from the pro-life movement that RU-
486 is dangerous are not based on the safety record of the drug.
The viewpoint traces how the safety record for RU-486 has been
largely ignored by the pro-life movement, and maintains that the
battle over the approval of RU-486 is about politics, not safety.*
The Nation, *founded in 1865, is a weekly journal of opinion,
featuring analysis on politics and culture.*

As you read, consider the following questions:

1. What "important medical professional organizations"
   approved mifepristone, according to the viewpoint?

2. According to the viewpoint, what percentage of U. S. women said they would recommend RU-486 to a friend in one clinical trail?

3. How is mifepristone/RU-486 different from surgical abortion?

It took twelve years for the FDA [Food and Drug Administration] to approve mifepristone—also known as RU-486—and most of that time had less to do with medicine than with the politics of abortion. Still, the . . . decision was a tremendous victory for American women. In approving RU-486, the FDA showed that science and good sense can still carry the day, even in an election year.

The long delay may even backfire against the drug's opponents. In 1988, when mifepristone was legalized in France, it was a medical novelty as well as a political flashpoint. Today, it's been accepted in thirteen countries, including most of western Europe; it's been taken by more than a half-million women and studied, it sometimes seems, by almost as many researchers. By the end of the approval process, the important medical professional organizations—the AMA [American Medical Association], the American Medical Women's Association, the American College of Obstetricians and Gynecologists—had given mifepristone their blessing; impressive percentages of ob-gyns and family practitioners said they would consider prescribing it; thousands of US women had taken it in clinical trials and given it high marks, with 97 percent in one study saying they would recommend it to a friend. Against this background of information and experience, the antichoicers' attempt to raise fears about the drug's safety sounds desperate and insincere.

A More Acceptable Alternative

In a normal country, RU-486 would simply be another abortion method, its use a matter of personal preference (in France

The At-Home Abortion Option

Studies from the USA have reported high efficacy and good acceptability of medical abortion in the home setting [using drugs such as low-dose mifepristone and misoprostol]. The availability of medical abortion at home allows the abortion process to be carried out in the privacy of a familiar environment and provides an additional choice for women. It also has cost-saving implications for the health service provider.

A pilot study was carried out in Scotland with women self-administering sublingual misoprostol at home to assess the efficacy, feasibility and acceptability of medical abortion at home. This study involved 49 women undergoing medical abortion under 56 days' gestation. Of these, 48 women aborted at home. While 98% of women expressed satisfaction with the procedure, 89% of women were happy to recommend the procedure to a friend. These findings suggest the feasibility and acceptability of the home medical abortion; however, they need to be assessed in the context of a randomized controlled trial. . . . In a multicenter trial organized by the WHO [World Health Organization] only 32% of women preferred to have medical abortion at home (41% in Caucasians, 21% in the Chinese population and 34% in other Asian populations). Medical abortion at home was preferred by women over 30 years of age and women with previous abortions or pregnancies. However, a higher percentage of women in the USA preferred to have medical abortion at home.

Manisha Mathur and Premila Ashok, "An Overview of Medical Abortion Using Low-Dose Mifepristone and Misoprostol," Expert Review of Obstetrics & Gynecology, *May 2007.*

it's the choice of 20 percent of women who have abortions, while in Britain only 6 percent opt for it). But in the United States, where abortion clinics are besieged by fanatics and providers wear bulletproof vests, mifepristone's main significance lies in its potential to widen access to abortion, especially in those 86 percent of US counties that possess no abortion clinic, by making it private—doctors unable or unwilling to perform surgical abortions could prescribe it, and women could take it at home.

It is unlikely, however, that Mifeprex, as the drug will be known when it comes on the market, will prove to be the magic bullet that ends the war on abortion by depriving antichoice activists of identifiable targets. The nation has been retreating from *Roe v. Wade* for a quarter-century, and a good portion of the patchwork of state and local regulations intended to discourage surgical abortion will apply to Mifeprex as well: parental notification and consent laws (thirty-two states), waiting periods (nineteen states), biased counseling and cumbersome reporting and zoning requirements. States in which antichoicers control the legislatures will surely rush to encumber Mifeprex with hassles, and small-town and rural physicians in particular may find it hard to prescribe Mifeprex without alerting antichoice activists. Doctors are a cautious bunch, and the anticipated flood of new providers may turn out to be a trickle, at least at first. Abortion rights activists should also brace themselves for a backlash from their hardcore foes: Just after the FDA's decision was announced, a Catholic priest crashed his car into an Illinois abortion clinic and hacked at the building with an ax.

But in the long run, Mifeprex will make abortion more acceptable. In poll after poll, Americans have said that when it comes to terminating a pregnancy, the earlier the better. Mifeprex, which has been approved for the first forty-nine days after a woman's last menstrual period—when the embryo's size varies from a pencil point to a grain of rice—

may well prove not to arouse the same kinds of anxieties and moral qualms as surgical abortion. Then, too, Americans are used to taking pills. That, of course, is what the antichoicers are afraid of.

"*RU-486 has caused a tremendously high rate of adverse events relative to the number of women who have taken the drug.*"

RU-486 Is Not Safe

Michelle Gress

When four deaths in 2005 were attributed to the abortion pill RU-486 (mifepristone), U.S. Congress began a review process of the drug and its approval. Michelle Gress argues in the following viewpoint that this review is long overdue and should result in the pulling of this drug from the U.S. market. Gress points out the dangers the drug presents for women who take it and notes that there is an unusually high number of complications associated with use of the drug when compared with the overall number of individuals who have taken it. Additionally, the author states that mifepristone has a mortality rate ten times that of surgical abortion. Gress is the director of operations for the Westchester Institute for Ethics & the Human Person and was counsel to the House Subcommittee on Criminal Justice, Drug Policy and Human Resources during the investigation of the Food and Drug Administration's approval of RU-486.

Michelle Gress, "'Safe' as a Car Accident: RU-486 Fallacies," *National Review Online*, August 22, 2007. Reproduced by permission.

As you read, consider the following questions:

1. What are some of the findings of the Congressional report *FDA and RU-486: Lowering the Standard for Women's Health* with regards to the dangers mifepristone poses to women, as Michelle Gress reports?

2. For what two reasons did RU-486 not meet the FDA's Subpart H criteria, according to Gress?

3. In Gress's viewpoint, what known adverse health effects did the FDA report to be associated with the use of RU-486?

According to the *TIME* headline last week [August 2006], a new study finds that the abortion pill RU-486 is "safe." The only drug approved by the FDA [Food and Drug Administration] that is designed to end human life, rather than improve it, "doesn't increase risks" said the *Chicago Tribune* headline.

These headlines take deception in journalism to a whole new level. During the last Congress, I served as counsel to the House subcommittee on drug policy that investigated the FDA's approval of RU-486. Anyone who seriously examines the highly irregular approval process and the serious adverse events associated with this drug can only conclude that it poses a deadly danger to women and should be removed from the market.

Questionable FDA Approval

Following confirmation by the FDA in late 2005 that four women died from a rare bacterial infection after taking RU-486, Congressman Mark Souder, then-chairman of the House Subcommittee on Criminal Justice, Drug Policy and Human Resources, initiated a year-long investigation of how the FDA was handling RU-486 and addressing the adverse events associated with it. The subcommittee gathered thousands of documents from the FDA, conducted dozens of interviews, and held a congressional hearing, "RU-486: Demonstrating a Low Standard for Women's Health?" Ultimately, the subcommittee published an extensive staff report on the drug, recommending its immediate removal from the market.

The report, *FDA and RU-486: Lowering the Standard for Women's Health*, summarizes a mountain of evidence about this drug's serious and unpredictable danger to women, detailing the reasons that the drug should be immediately withdrawn from the market. Here are just some highlights: RU-486 was fraudulently approved; it has caused the deaths of at least eight women (that are known); and it is at least ten times deadlier than its surgical alternative.

RU-486 is actually a two-drug combination that first blocks nutrition from the developing embryo, which kills it, then causes the uterus to contract and expel the contents. It was approved in the waning days of the [Bill] Clinton presidency under a highly unusual and specialized federal provision called Subpart H, which applies only to drugs that treat "serious or life-threatening illnesses and that provide a meaningful therapeutic benefit" over existing treatments.

A Poor Record of Safety

RU-486 doesn't even come close to meeting the Subpart H criteria: A normal pregnancy is not a serious or life-threatening illness (RU-486 is contraindicated for ectopic pregnancies); and surgical alternatives are safer for the mother. In short, FDA violated its own regulations to approve RU-486. (The advocacy group Judicial Watch has a detailed report on the Clinton administration's drive to approve RU-486; and a Citizens Petition filed against the FDA on behalf of Concerned Women for America, the American Association of Pro-Life Obstetricians and Gynecologists, and Christian Medical Association offers a comprehensive account of the approval violations committed on behalf of RU-486 approval.)

RU-486 has caused a tremendously high rate of adverse events relative to the number of women who have taken the drug. As of last year [2006], when the FDA provided information to the subcommittee for its investigation, RU-486 had caused the deaths of at least eight women, nine life-threatening incidents, 232 hospitalizations, 116 blood transfusions, and 88 cases of infection. In total, we knew of more than 1070 adverse event cases associated with RU-486, out of only 575,000 prescriptions at most. This is even more alarming in light of the fact that adverse event reporting is notoriously low for any drug, much less a drug associated with abortion, for which reporting is expected to be even lower.

Finally, as explained in detail in the *New England Journal of Medicine*, RU-486 abortion (sometimes called "medical abortion") is at least ten times more fatal than its surgical alternative. The figure, based on the most conservative numbers available, compares deaths from RU-486 abortion (a rate of 1 per 100,000) to surgical abortion before eight weeks (a rate of 0.1 per 100,000).

Now, just a few interesting facts about the business and manufacturing of this drug: Danco, the company that imports and distributes RU-486 (under the trade name of Mifeprex), is not a U.S. company, but is based in the Cayman Islands; RU-486 is its only product (making a voluntary withdrawal highly unlikely); and Danco imports RU-486 from that paragon of safe-product production, China.

RU-486 Should Be Banned

So what are the options for actually withdrawing this drug from the market? There is a bill in the House that would suspend approval of RU-486 pending a Comptroller General review of the FDA's initial approval. But approval could be reinstated after a favorable Comptroller General review. The FDA has authority, under a few provisions, for withdrawing a drug unilaterally, such as when a drug cannot be used safely despite restrictions, but it's highly unlikely the FDA would pursue this course of action. The best current option for withdrawal of RU-486 rests with the Secretary of Health and Human Services, who has "Imminent Hazard" authority to remove a drug from the market under certain criteria (such as the unpredictability and severity of adverse events associated with a drug).

Returning to the mendacious headlines claiming RU-486 is "safe," the careful reader will note that the study prompting this recent PR [public relations] blitz lauding the abortion pill was not about the safety of RU-486 as a drug, or even as a form of abortion. The study was a comparison of subsequent pregnancy outcomes among women who had prior abortions, concluding that there was no difference between surgical or medical abortion on the impact on subsequent pregnancy.

However, abortion in general poses some risk to subsequent pregnancy; so to say there is no difference in long-term risk after having a medical versus surgical abortion is like saying there is no difference in long-term risk after getting into a traffic accident in a sedan versus a motorcycle. It ignores the fact that traffic accidents are dangerous, and motorcycle accidents are much more deadly.

> "Ask anyone who has had an abortion if
> it has affected her in a negative way
> mentally, and she will most likely tell
> you that it did."

Post-Abortion Emotional Problems Harm Women

Corinne Cords

Having an abortion increases the likelihood that a woman will experience mental disorders, according to Corinne Cords in the following viewpoint. Cords contends that multiple studies have proven that abortion has a negative impact on a woman's mental health and well-being. In addition, she accuses abortion providers and pro-choice supporters of suppressing this information so that they can continue to provide the risky procedure. Cords is the executive director of Self-Evident Truth, an organization dedicated to educating the public about the horrors of abortion and providing pro-life supporters with the tools they need to work in the fight to ban abortion.

As you read, consider the following questions:

1. How does Corinne Cords define post-abortion syndrome?

Corinne Cords, "The Eye on Abortion: Used and Abused: How Women Are Mistreated by the Abortion Industry, Part 2," *Self-Evident Truth*, December 2007. Copyright © 2007. www.selfevidenttruth.org. Reproduced by permission.

2. What are some of the symptoms Cords claims post-abortive women experience?

3. According to Cords, how has the American Psychological Association responded to claims that women experience mental disorders following abortion?

If ever there were a cover-up, it would be the way the abortion industry (and its accomplices) stifles any legitimate studies that reveal how abortion so negatively affects women. Planned Parenthood, the Guttmacher Institute, and almost every major health organization in America reject the notion that abortion causes harm to a woman's mental health.

Ask anyone who has had an abortion if it has affected her in a negative way mentally, and she will most likely tell you that it did. It doesn't take stacks of research to know that. I have spoken with some hard-core pro-aborts who have received abortions. Trying not to cry, with anger in their eyes, they claimed their abortions did not affect them negatively and that they had no regrets. Not very convincing.

Pro-abort college students have commented to me many times saying, "No one *likes* abortion." My response has always been, "And why is that?" To which they typically replied in one form or another, "Because it is . . . ending the . . . life of the . . . fetus." (This, after they usually just debated with me for 10 minutes about how the unborn are *not* human!) If the unborn are not human beings then why doesn't anyone *like* abortion?

I would support abortion if it were like getting an appendix removed, or a tooth pulled, but it's not. And *everyone* knows that. That is why the existence of post-abortion syndrome is often times a very real result from abortion.

However, pro-aborts continue to assert the claim that abortion is "safe" for women, backing it up with outrageous rhetoric and unreliable studies. . . .

Identifying the Negative Mental Health Impacts

Before we go any further, let's define our terms. Post-abortion syndrome is a form of post-traumatic stress disorder. People often develop post-traumatic stress disorder after experiencing something very traumatic in their lives. In this case, that would be abortion.

In brief, some of the symptoms encountered by post-abortive women are:

Sexual Dysfunction	Suicide Attempts or Thoughts of Suicide
Alcohol Abuse	Drug Abuse
Increased Smoking	Eating Disorders
Child Neglect or Abuse	Divorce and Chronic Relationship Problems
Repeat Abortions	Nervous Disorders
Sleep Disturbances	Regret About Abortion Decision

As you will see later, there is plenty of evidence to back up the existence of these symptoms in post-abortive women and girls. Since business would go down dramatically for Planned Parenthood if word of this got out to the public, they have to come up with a way to get around it. The way of the serpent, used way back in the Garden of Eden, is one of their favorites.

Why do I always pick on Planned Parenthood? I single them out not only because they kill the greatest number of unborn children in America, but also because they have made an art of deceiving the public. They state blatant lies as if they were truth and never even flinch. Maybe they have even talked *themselves* into believing their own lies, but it does not work on the informed pro-lifer! Let's begin by looking at what Planned Parenthood has to say about how abortion affects the mental health of women and girls.

Abortion Is Not Therapeutic

Not only does Planned Parenthood (PP) refuse to admit the damage abortion does to women mentally, they actually claim abortion does just the *opposite*! On PP's Web site, they state the following under the heading "Abortion as a Positive Coping Mechanism":

- "For most women who have had abortions, the procedure represents a maturing experience, a successful coping with a personal crisis situation. . ."

- "Up to 98 percent of the women who have abortions have no regrets and would make the same choice again in similar circumstances."

- "Women who have had one abortion do not suffer adverse psychological effects. In fact, as a group, they have higher self-esteem, greater feelings of worth and capableness, and fewer feelings of failure than do women who have had *no* abortions. . ."

- "The positive relationship of abortion to well-being may be due in part to abortion's role in controlling fertility and its relationship to coping resources."

There are *so* many things that could be said about these statements that I could write the rest of my newsletter on them alone! Since I will address most of those comments in some form later in this newsletter, I will just comment on one point they *tried* to make. In the third point listed, it is beyond belief that they would say that if a girl receives an abortion her self-esteem will increase, she will feel more worthy, capable and like less of a failure than if she had *never received an abortion*! Now abortion is *therapeutic*! I know many women and men who have dealt with abortion, and if you do too, you realize how absurd that assertion really is! It is always one of the most raw, sensitive memories they have.

Later, in the same article on PP's Web site, they even go on to claim that when women are denied abortion they are more likely to have "genetically malformed children"!

And what about other options? Could there be a better option than abortion? How about adoption? PP tries to scare women away from that option by saying that most women believe it will cause them "even greater emotional trauma than abortion." Childbearing? Look out! Postpartum depression will overtake this woman for sure! This will also most likely cause her child to have "impaired mental or motor development, low self-esteem, and behavioral difficulties." Clearly, abortion is the best option according to PP.

They go on to say that if abortion *does* bring any guilt or depression, it is due to pre-existing mental health conditions, not because of abortion itself. But is that true? Is there no such thing as post-abortion syndrome?

Study Shows a Link Between Abortion and Mental Disorder

There have been several credible studies that made strong cases that abortion causes post-abortion syndrome, but one study that came out in 2005 deserves serious attention. David Reardon, the director of the Elliot Institute, wrote a great summary of the study. The excerpts below were taken from that article (it is lengthy but highly informative!):

A study in New Zealand that tracked approximately *500 women from birth to 25 years of age* has confirmed that young women who have abortions subsequently experience elevated rates of suicidal behaviors, depression, substance abuse, anxiety, and other mental problems.

Most significantly, the researchers—led by Professor David M. Fergusson, who is the director of the longitudinal Christchurch Health and Development Study—found that *the higher rate of subsequent mental problems could not be explained by any pre-pregnancy differences in mental health, which had been regularly evaluated over the course of the 25-year study.*

Findings Surprise Pro-Choice Researchers

According to Fergusson, the researchers had undertaken the study anticipating that they would be able to confirm the view that any problems found after abortion would be traceable to mental health problems that had existed before the abortion. At first glance, it appeared that their data would confirm this hypothesis. The data showed that women who became pregnant before age 25 were more likely to have experienced family dysfunction and adjustment problems, were more likely to have left home at a young age, and were more likely to have entered a cohabiting relationship.

However, when these and many other factors were taken into account, the findings showed that women who had abortions were still significantly more likely to experience mental health problems. Thus, the data contradicted the hypothesis that prior mental illness or other "pre-disposing" factors could explain the differences.

"We know what people were like before they became pregnant," Fergusson told the *New Zealand Herald*. "We take into account their social background, education, ethnicity, previous mental health, exposure to sexual abuse, and a whole mass of factors."

The data persistently pointed toward the politically unwelcome conclusion that abortion may itself be the cause of subsequent mental health problems. So Fergusson presented his results to New Zealand's Abortion Supervisory Committee, which is charged with ensuring that abortions in that country are conducted in accordance with all the legal requirements. According to the *New Zealand Herald*, the committee told Fergusson that it would be "undesirable to publish the results in their 'unclarified' state."

Despite his own pro-choice political beliefs, Fergusson responded to the committee with a letter stating that it would be "scientifically irresponsible" to suppress the findings simply because they touched on an explosive political issue.

In an interview about the findings with an Australian radio host, Fergusson stated: "I remain pro-choice. I am not religious. I am an atheist and a rationalist. The findings did surprise me, but the results appear to be very robust because they persist across a series of disorders and a series of ages. . . . Abortion is a traumatic life event; that is, it involves loss, it involves grief, it involves difficulties. And the trauma may, in fact, predispose people to having mental illness."

Journals Reject the Politically Incorrect Results

The research team of the Christchurch Health and Development Study is used to having its studies on health and human development accepted by the top medical journals on first submission. After all, the collection of data from birth to adulthood of 1,265 children born in Christchurch is one of the most long-running and valuable longitudinal studies in the world. But this study was the first from the experienced research team that touched on the contentious issue of abortion.

Fergusson said the team "went to four journals, which is very unusual for us—we normally get accepted the first time." Finally, the fourth journal accepted the study for publication.

Although he still holds a pro-choice view, Fergusson believes women and doctors should not blindly accept the unsupported claim that abortion is generally harmless or beneficial to women.

"This New Zealand study, with its unsurpassed controls for possible alternative explanations, confirms the findings of several recent studies linking abortion to higher rates of psychiatric hospitalization, depression, generalized anxiety disorder, substance abuse, suicidal tendencies, poor bonding with and parenting of later children, and sleep disorders," he said. "It should inevitably lead to a change in the standard of care offered to women facing problem pregnancies."

Men's Response to Abortion Is Largely Ignored

In contrast to the growing body of research concerning the psychological impact of abortion on women, relatively few studies have addressed the psychological impact of abortion on men. Likely reasons for this paucity of research include societal, political, and legal factors. Society continues to view abortion as a women's issue. Both the media and politicians portray abortion as being of consequence to women only. Therefore, many people give little thought or attention to male partners' reactions to elective abortion. Legally, the inclusion of men in the abortion debate would severely complicate the issue. If men were accorded legal rights in abortion decisions (as they currently are in both adoption decisions and those concerning frozen embryos), there would be enormous challenges in deciding between the competing legal claims of fathers and mothers. Furthermore, due to the time apt to be spent in litigation, women may be unable to obtain abortion until later in pregnancy which would significantly increase the risks of the procedure. . . .

Catherine T. Coyle,
"Men and Abortion: A Review of Empirical Reports
Concerning the Impact of Abortion on Men,"
Internet Journal of Mental Health, *vol. 3, issue 2, 2007.*

According to Reardon, the best available medical evidence shows that it is easier for a woman to adjust to the birth of an unintended child than it is to adjust to the emotional turmoil caused by an abortion.

"We are social beings, so it is easier for people to adjust to having a new relationship in one's life than to adjust to the loss of a relationship," he said. "In the context of abortion, adjusting to the loss is especially difficult if there [are] any unresolved feelings of attachment, grief, or guilt."

Fergusson also believes that the same rules that apply to other medical treatments should apply to abortion. "If we were talking about an antibiotic or an asthma risk, and someone reported adverse reactions, people would be advocating further research to evaluate risk," he said in the *New Zealand Herald*. "I can see no good reason why the same rules don't apply to abortion."

Pro-Choice Advocates Deny Evidence

How does PP respond to this rock solid study? They say on their Web site that this study is flawed because "researchers admitted to not asking subjects if they had previous psychiatric illnesses." But that makes no sense whatsoever since the subjects were followed from *birth* and researchers knew every aspect of their lives, including their "previous mental health." So I can only conclude that PP is once again lying to deny the evidence.

PP also cites the American Psychological Association's (APA) stance on abortion as proof that post-abortion syndrome does not exist. They state on their Web site:

> In 1989, a panel of experts assembled by the American Psychological Association (APA) concluded unanimously that legal abortion "does not create psychological hazards for most women undergoing the procedure." The panel noted that, since approximately 21 percent of all U.S. women have had an abortion, if severe emotional reactions were common there would be an epidemic of women seeking psychological treatment. There is no evidence of such an epidemic.

But is that the case?

In 2003, a study was published in the *Canadian Medical Association Journal* that showed that evidence of increased psychological treatment among post-abortive women *does* exist. The medical records of 56,741 California Medicaid patients were reviewed, and it was revealed that women who had abortions were 2.6 times more likely than delivering women to be hospitalized for psychiatric treatment within 90 days following abortion or delivery. Rates of psychiatric treatment remained much higher for at least four years. The most common diagnosis was depressive psychosis.

A Conspiracy of Misinformation

How has the APA responded to the evidence in these studies? According to the Elliot Institute, one of the world's foremost post-abortion research groups, the spokesperson for the APA, Dr. Nancy Felipe Russo, gave a shocking response to Warren Throckmorton, a columnist for the *Washington Times*. Russo said the Christchurch study (the first study cited above) would have no effect on the APA's position because, "To pro-choice advocates, mental health effects are not relevant to the legal context of arguments to restrict access to abortion." Below is more on that from the Elliot Institute:

> In the first draft of Throckmorton's column, which he sent for comment to another expert on abortion research, Dr. David Reardon of the Springfield, IL-based Elliot Institute, Russo was quoted more bluntly, saying, "it doesn't matter what the evidence says." Throckmorton and Russo subsequently agreed to the clarification of her statement as it appeared in the *Washington Times*.

> According to Reardon, an author of several of the studies on abortion that have been ignored by the APA, Russo's statements "confirm the complaint of critics that the APA's briefs to the Supreme Court and state legislatures are really about promoting a view about civil rights, not science. Toward this end, the APA has set up task forces and divisions that include only psychologists who share the same bias in favor of abortion."

Reardon believes the APA's task forces on abortion have actually served to stifle rather than encourage research. "When researchers like Fergusson or myself publish data showing abortion is linked to mental health problems, members of the APA's abortion policy police rush forward to tell the public to ignore our findings because they are completely out of line with their own 'consensus' statements which are positioned as the APA's official interpretation of the meaningful research on abortion."

Isn't the job of the APA to give reliable guidance about what is beneficial or dangerous to American's mental health? If the APA looks at the abortion issue from a political standpoint, how can they make a position statement that sounds like it is based on *science*? Is that fair to those who look to them for guidance? Here again is their official position: Legal abortion "does not create psychological hazards for most women undergoing the procedure." When the APA refuses to accept evidence that proves abortion *is* hazardous, but make a statement claiming the opposite, that is nothing short of lying to the public. This conspiracy of misinformation is only hurting more and more women and girls who would probably like to know the truth about abortion before going through with one.

The Resolve to Continue the Fight

There is so much more that could be said about this topic, but I have to stop before this newsletter turns into a book!

After seeing what is only the tip of the iceberg of the evidence supporting the fact that post-abortion syndrome exists, I hope you have come to see that it is a very real trauma women suffer. I encourage you to visit the Elliot Institute's Web site at www.afterabortion.org and read up further on this topic. There are a myriad of other studies and articles to read there as well!

Please pray that these little known facts about abortion would become more widely known, and that women would turn away from abortion as a result! Please also keep SET [Self-Evident Truth] in your prayers as we continue to work to battle abortion on a daily basis!

> *"Anti-reproductive rights activists are using poor science to reposition their strategy from a fetally focused platform to a mother-focused 'abortion hurts women' argument."*

Post-Abortion Emotional Problems Are Rare

Julia R. Steinberg, Beth Jordan, and Elisa S. Wells

The post-procedure effects of abortion on women are hotly contested. In the viewpoint that follows, Julia R. Steinberg, Beth Jordan, and Elisa S. Wells argue that the evidence reported in study after study supports only one conclusion: Abortion is not a catalyst for mental health problems in women. The authors present information from two recent studies confirming that no connection exists between the two, and they also outline the methodological flaws in the studies supporting the connection. Additionally, they worry that the intense focus on the relationship between abortion and mental health problems distracts researchers from investigating the actual causes of the disorders. Steinberg holds a doctorate in psychology and is currently a research fellow at the Bixby Center for Global Reproductive Health at the University of

Julia R. Steinberg, Beth Jordan, and Elisa S. Wells, "Science Prevails: Abortion and Mental Health," *Contraception*, vol. 79, February 2009, pp. 81–82. Copyright © 2009 Elsevier B.V. All rights reserved. Reprinted with permission from Elsevier.

California, San Francisco. Jordan is a doctor and medical director of the Association of Reproductive Health Professionals (ARHP), and Wells is the program consultant for the ARHP.

As you read, consider the following questions:

1. According to Julia R. Steinberg, Beth Jordan, and Elisa S. Wells, why is it impossible to conduct a study determining the causal relationship between abortion and poor mental health?

2. The authors claim that research concerning mental health and abortion has failed to consider what possible impact of abortion on mental health?

3. What three messages do the authors believe can be taken from sound scientific research?

Politics and ideology have long battled—and often trumped—the scientific evidence surrounding the safety of abortion. This has been particularly true of the issue of abortion and mental health. Although major organizations, including the American Psychological Association, have been firm in their assertions that abortion does not harm mental health, antichoice activists have used questionable science to push the concept of "post-abortion syndrome" into both clinical practice and law. For years, this specious claim has been fueling attempts in the United States to legislate that women be informed of this "risk" or denied access to abortion to protect them from "risk." The U.S. Supreme Court cited the possibility of women experiencing "regret ... [which can be followed by] severe depression and loss of esteem" after abortion in its decision to uphold the Partial-Birth Abortion Ban Act (*Gonzales v. Carhart*), all the while acknowledging that there are "no reliable data to measure the phenomenon."

Fortunately, recent reviews of the scientific literature reinforce what many reproductive health care providers already know: Evidence for the claim that abortion negatively affects a woman's mental health is lacking. How well we as reproductive health providers and advocates are able to convey this positive message to patients, the public, and policy makers will depend, in part, on how well we ourselves understand the findings and feel confident in their scientific integrity. Here, we examine the details of some recent analyses, the strength of their scientific underpinnings, and their implications for clinical practice.

Understanding the Evidence

Two recent reviews of the scientific research on abortion and mental health have come to similar conclusions. One by [researchers Vignelta E.] Charles, [Chelsea B. Polis, Srinivas K. Sridhara, and Robert W. Blum published in the December 2008 *Contraception*] concluded that "... the highest quality studies had findings that were mostly neutral, suggesting few, if any, differences between women who had abortions and their respective comparison groups in terms of mental health sequelae. Conversely, studies with the most flawed methodology found negative mental health sequelae of abortion." The other review, by the American Psychological Association abortion task force [published in August 2008], similarly found that, to date, the most rigorous research shows that having a first-trimester abortion does not increase a woman's risk for negative mental health outcomes compared with delivering the pregnancy among adult women who have an unintended pregnancy.

Conducting a study to determine whether having an abortion *causes* poor mental health outcomes is not possible because women cannot be randomly assigned to have an abortion or a delivery. Thus, as [psychologist Nancy E.] Adler discussed, all research studies comparing the mental health effects of women who have abortions with those of women who have deliveries contain methodological flaws in answering this

173

question. Instead, what can be answered is whether there is evidence (or not) for the claim that abortion leads to negative mental health effects.

Designing Studies to Collect Reliable Results

While Adler stated that placing less faith in the most poorly designed research—those using case studies, highly selected samples, having no standardized or replicable method of data collection or analysis—is reasonable, such research cannot be ignored because it is introduced into state legislatures or courts as a reason to ban abortions or to require informed consent. For instance, the claim that abortion leads to severe depression and loss of self-esteem was a justification for upholding the partial-birth abortion procedure ban. In such a climate, in which strong scientific evidence is dismissed and the most unscientific research is used for political agenda, the advancement of science may be thwarted: Scholars must continue to consider the claim that abortion leads to negative mental health outcomes in designing their research, despite a growing consensus that lacks evidence for such a claim. As a result, little research considers potential positive mental health aspects of having an abortion. A woman may feel positively about her ability to exercise control of her reproductive decisions, or positive emotions may arise from the belief that her other children will have more opportunities because of her decision. Furthermore, for the few women who do experience negative mental health outcomes after an abortion, it may be less negative for them than if they had chosen to deliver their pregnancy.

It remains crucial to continue to conduct well-designed research examining the psychological outcomes of abortion because the findings from poorly designed research are widely disseminated to the public, used in setting policy and presented as scientifically sound when they are not. An example of a study by [researchers Jesse R.] Cougle, [David C. Reardon, and Priscilla K. Coleman published in a 2005 *Journal of Anxiety Disorders*] used for such purposes concluded that "... findings highlight the clinical relevance of exploring reproductive history [i.e., abortion history] in therapeutic efforts to assist women seeking relief from anxiety." Its conclusions were drawn from a study using particularly poor methodological and data analysis techniques. First, it excluded women who had subsequent abortions from the delivery group but not from the abortion group. In biasing the delivery group, the authors increased their chances of confirming their claims. Second, they excluded women who experienced a period of anxiety prior to their first pregnancy. Excluding women who experienced previous anxiety is an inappropriate statistical technique to control for previous anxiety. Instead, a covariate that controls for whether or not a woman experienced previous anxiety should be included in the model. Finally, they excluded important contextual variables (e.g., violence history) that have been shown to be associated with both abortion history and negative mental health outcomes.

Examining Alternative Causes of Anxiety

In a reanalysis of the data used by Cougle et al., [researchers Julia R.] Steinberg and [Nancy F.] Russo controlled for the number of subsequent abortions, and included experience of previous anxiety symptoms and having been raped in their analysis. There was no difference in the prevalence of post-pregnancy anxiety between women who terminated and those who delivered their first pregnancy. Instead, pre-pregnancy anxiety and having been raped were strongly related to post-pregnancy anxiety, regardless of pregnancy outcome—consistent with existing research. Additionally, in a second study, Steinberg and Russo found that having multiple abortions was associated with both negative mental health outcomes and violence experience (e.g., having been raped, molested or held

The Inability to Affirm Abortion's Harm

Despite years of trying, antiabortion activists failed to gain any traction with the nation's major medical groups in alleging that abortion posed a direct threat to women's health, especially their mental health, so they turned to the political process to legitimize their claims. In 1987, they convinced President [Ronald] Reagan to direct U.S. Surgeon General C. Everett Koop to analyze the health effects of abortion and submit a report to the president. As Koop had been appointed to his position in no small part because of his antiabortion views, both pro-choice and antiabortion factions believed the outcome to be preordained. (An eminent pediatric surgeon as well as an outspoken abortion foe, Koop had no prior experience or background in public health; both public health and pro-choice advocates in Congress vehemently opposed his appointment, delaying his confirmation by several months.)

Koop reviewed the scientific and medical literature and consulted with a wide range of experts and advocacy groups on both sides of the issue. Yet, after 15 months, no report was forthcoming. Rather, on January 9, 1989, Koop wrote a letter to the president explaining that he would not be issuing a report at all because "the scientific studies do not provide conclusive data about the health effects of abortion on women." Koop apparently was referring to the effects of abortion on mental health, because his letter essentially dismissed any doubts about the physical safety of the procedure.

Susan A. Cohen,
"Abortion and Mental Health: Myths and Realities,"
Guttmacher Policy Review, *Summer 2006.*

captive/threatened with a weapon/kidnapped). When analyses were conducted that included both violence experience and having multiple abortions (versus not), having multiple abortions was no longer associated with a greater likelihood of having negative mental health outcomes. Violence experience, however, remained associated with negative mental health outcomes. The same factors that increase a woman's chance of experiencing more negative post-abortion psychological experiences also increase her chance of negative reactions to other types of stressful life events, including childbirth. The focus on abortion as the *cause* of negative mental health outcomes has detracted from other known causes of or predispositions for negative mental health outcomes: violence and previous mental health. For instance, rather than focusing on the negative psychological outcomes of abortion, Steinberg and Russo's results suggest the need for clinicians to provide women who have abortions or unintended pregnancies with referrals to services that help victims of violence. Scientific progress in understanding the experience of women's reproductive decisions does not have to be stunted by those with a political agenda.

Utilizing the Data to Craft an Appropriate Response

The burgeoning data trend is that abortion does not harm women. For the millions of women already dealing with complex emotions as they face an unintended pregnancy, the good news is that they can thoroughly examine all available options for themselves and their families without the additional risk of worrying about developing anxiety or other negative mental health sequelae should they choose abortion.

The messages from sound scientific research for health care practitioners and public policy crafters are clear:

- Health care providers need to screen for violence. Screening for violence could certainly have an impact on picking up treatable anxiety as well as helping prevent unintended pregnancies.

- Health care providers should exercise and strengthen their critical appraisal skills. By analyzing the data and being clear and well-versed on the methodological biases and design flaws apparent in studies, clinicians can be confident of their medical practice, instill deepened confidence in their patients, and help sway a confused public when faced with ideologically divisive matters.

- Reproductive health policy and legislation must be based on the best available science. Evidence-based science serves to acknowledge the complicated emotional terrain that many women face when confronting an unintended pregnancy and provides them access to sound and unbiased information, enabling them to make their own decisions.

As reproductive health care advocates, researchers and providers of comprehensive and compassionate care, it goes without saying that only the highest quality studies should inform their clinical practice and public policy. But anti-reproductive rights activists are using poor science to reposition their strategy from a fetally focused platform to a mother-focused "abortion hurts women" argument.

Periodical Bibliography

The following articles have been selected to supplement the diverse views presented in this chapter.

E. Joanne Angelo	"The Aftermath of Abortion Trauma," *Human Life Review*, Spring 2007.
Erika Bachiochi	"How Abortion Hurts Women: The Hard Proof," *Crisis*, June 2005.
Nicholas Bakalar	"Breast Cancer Not Linked to Abortion, Study Says," *New York Times*, April 24, 2007.
Deborah Bartz and Alisa Goldberg	"Medication Abortion," *Clinical Obstetrics & Gynecology*, June 2009.
Sarah Blustain	"Beyond Regret," *American Prospect*, July-August 2007.
Patrick S. Carroll	"The Breast Cancer Epidemic: Modeling and Forecasts Based on Abortion and Other Risk Factors," *Journal of American Physicians & Surgeons*, Fall 2007.
Laura Echevarria	"RU-486: A Bitter Pill," *Human Life Review*, Summer-Fall 2006.
Carolyn Sayre	"The Abortion Pill Could Prevent Cancer," *TIME*, December 3, 2006.
Caitlin Shannon and Beverly Winikoff	"How Much Supervision Is Necessary for Women Taking Mifepristone and Misoprostol for Early Medical Abortion?" *Women's Health*, March 2008.
Stephanie Simon	"New Front in Abortion Battle," *Wall Street Journal*, August 12, 2008.

For Further Discussion

Chapter 1

1. In his viewpoint, Jeff Jones contends that abortion is wrong because murdering is wrong. On the other hand, *Revolution* argues that abortion is morally justifiable because it often saves the life of the woman, and a woman should not be forced to make decisions based on government mandates. Whose view do you find more convincing? Do you think that a fetus's life should be judged the same as an adult's life? Is a grown woman's life more important than that of an unborn baby? Justify your answer using quotations from the viewpoints.

2. Often the issue of human rights is central to the debate about abortion. Reread the third and fourth viewpoints in the first chapter. After considering the arguments, do you believe that the issue of human rights is important to the abortion debate? Should an unborn fetus be considered a human and granted rights equal to those of an adult? Use the text from both viewpoints to provide support for your view.

3. *Genocide* is a term that has recently been applied to abortion, often by members of the pro-life community. Those who are pro-choice believe the use of this term is inflammatory and inaccurate. Those employing the term to describe abortion contend it is the only appropriate word to use. After reading the viewpoints by Meredith Eugene Hunt and Cathleen Kaveny, create your own working definition of genocide. Considering your definition, does genocide accurately describe abortion, or does it detract from other instances of genocide? Compare abortion to

other acts of genocide to support your answer, conducting additional research as necessary.

Chapter 2

1. Susan E. Wills contends that abortions conducted in the second and third trimesters of pregnancy are "a bridge too far"—meaning a step beyond what most supporters of abortion consider a reasonable application of abortion laws. After reading the viewpoints by Wills and the Abortion Rights Coalition of Canada, explain whether you think there are degrees of abortion that should be regulated by different laws. Cite arguments from the viewpoints to support your answer.

2. Reread the viewpoints on parental consent laws in this chapter. Then explain the extent to which you think parents should be involved in their children's decisions to seek abortion. Michael New suggests that parents deserve the right to influence their pregnant daughters' decisions, while Diana Philip maintains that such involvement impinges on the rights of the daughters. Whose rights do you think should be paramount in this argument? Explain using evidence and arguments from the viewpoints.

Chapter 3

1. Retired archbishop Daniel W. Kucera argues that legalized abortion is the sign of a weak society, while Joyce Arthur states that it is the hallmark of a strong society. How do the two authors make their arguments? What logic do they use and what evidence do they claim? Whose assertions do you find more convincing? Can you think of examples outside the two viewpoints that shape your decision? Explain.

2. Examine the arguments of John R. Lott Jr. and Robert Wanderer. Both viewpoints suggest that legalized abortion has had an impact on crime rates in the United States,

but the authors differ on whether that impact has been positive or negative. Both claims are difficult to prove and depend on correlations of statistics over time. Do you believe either argument to be accurate? What proposals can you think of that might call into question the conclusions of one or both of the viewpoints?

Chapter 4

1. Both viewpoints concerning the possible connection between abortion and breast cancer claim that scientific fact either supports or debunks this link. Examine the evidence given in each article. Then, explain which view you find more compelling. Scan the Internet or periodicals to see if you can find more support for the viewpoint that you favor.

2. After reading the viewpoints in this chapter, decide what you think is the greatest risk to women who have abortions. Consider potential physical and mental trauma when answering the question. Are there ways to lessen these risks? Explain.

Organizations to Contact

The editors have compiled the following list of organizations concerned with the issues debated in this book. The descriptions are derived from materials provided by the organizations. All have publications or information available for interested readers. The list was compiled on the date of publication of the present volume; the information provided here may change. Be aware that many organizations take several weeks or longer to respond to inquiries, so allow as much time as possible.

Afterabortion.com
PASS Web site, Glen Burnie, MD   21060
e-mail: help@passhugs.com
Web site: www.afterabortion.com

Afterabortion.com is a Web site dedicated to providing support to women who have had abortions and are dealing with Post Abortion Stress Syndrome (PASS) following the procedure. The site takes no political stance on abortion. It offers a forum for women to discuss their personal experiences. Links to additional resources are provided.

Americans United for Life (AUL)
310 South Peoria Street, Suite 500, Chicago, IL   60607
(312) 568-4700 • fax: (312) 568-4747
Web site: www.aul.org

Founded in August 1971, prior to the *Roe v. Wade* Supreme Court decision, Americans United for Life (AUL) is the nation's oldest pro-life organization. AUL promotes pro-life ideals and policies from a non-denominational, interdisciplinary perspective. The organization believes that abortion harms women, men, and society and should be banned. Information about current local and national abortion legislation and ongoing pro-life activities sponsored by the organization is available on AUL's Web site.

Center for Bio-Ethical Reform (CBR)
PO Box 219, Lake Forest, CA   92609
(949) 206-0600
e-mail: info@cbrinfo.org
Web site: www.abortionno.org

The Center for Bio-Ethical Reform (CBR) seeks to expose the injustice of abortion through graphic representations. Its ultimate goal is a nationwide ban on abortion. The center's groups, the Reproductive "Choice" Campaign, the Genocide Awareness Project, Matthew 28:20, and AbortionNo, were formed to accomplish this goal. Each targets a particular community using arguments specific to that group and graphic abortion images. Information about these campaigns and other educational resources can be found on CBR's Web site.

The Coalition on Abortion/Breast Cancer
PO Box 957133, Hoffman Estates, IL   60195
(847) 421-4000
e-mail: response@abortionbreastcancer.com
Web site: www.abortionbreastcancer.com

The Coalition on Abortion/Breast Cancer provides scientific evidence showing a link between abortion and breast cancer, called the ABC link. The coalition's purpose is to ensure that the ABC link is publicized and fully studied, so women are educated about the risks associated with having an abortion. The coalition publishes press releases, a periodic newsletter, and links to additional information about recent studies exploring the ABC link on its Web site.

Guttmacher Institute
125 Maiden Lane, 7th Floor, New York, NY
(212) 248-1111 • fax: (212) 248-1951
Web site: www.guttmacher.org

The Guttmacher Institute's integrated program of social science research, public education, and policy analysis serves as the basis for the advancement of sexual and reproductive health for women and men around the globe. The institute welcomes the opinions and research of outside experts and encourages public debate about international health issues. The institute's specific goals include helping men and women make responsible family planning decisions, reducing the incidence of sexually transmitted disease, and ensuring that all individuals have access to safe abortions. Quarterly publications include *Perspectives on Sexual and Reproductive Health*, *International Perspectives on Sexual and Reproductive Health*, and *Guttmacher Policy Review*. Archives of these journals, reports, and information can be accessed online.

Life Education and Resource Network (LEARN)
PO Box 9400, Fayetteville, NC   28311
(910) 868-5327 • fax: (866) 253-4344
Web site: www.learninc.com

Life Education and Resource Network (LEARN) works to ensure that the U.S. African American community has the opportunity to thrive and that Judeo-Christian values serve as the basis for engaging in debate about bio-ethical issues. LEARN created www.blackgenocide.org to explore and address the high number of abortions sought by members of the African American community. The Web site provides information about the disproportionate number of African American women who have had abortions and suggests that this procedure is promoted within minority communities as a means of population control. Additional information can be obtained at www.blackgenocide.org.

NARAL Pro-Choice America
1156 Fifteenth Street NW, Suite 700, Washington, DC   20005
(202) 973-3000 • fax: (202) 973-3096
Web site: www.prochoiceamerica.org

Founded in 1969 as the National Association for the Repeal of Abortion Laws, NARAL Pro-Choice America is an advocate for women's reproductive rights. The organization works to ensure these rights are protected by supporting pro-choice policies and politicians; publishing information about abortion, birth control, and other reproduction topics; and organizing pro-choice campaigns at the grassroots level. Information about current activities and general information about abortion can be accessed on NARAL's Web site.

National Abortion Federation (NAF)
1660 L Street NW, Suite 450, Washington, DC   20036
(202) 667-5881 • fax: (202) 667-5890
e-mail: naf@prochoice.org
Web site: www.prochoice.org

As the professional organization of abortion providers in the United States, National Abortion Federation (NAF) supports these health professionals by providing training and other services to ensure that women have the best available information and care when making decisions about their reproductive health. NAF is pro-choice and believes that it is a woman's right to make decisions about her health and body without the interference of government regulations or mandates. The federation publishes guidelines for abortion providers, educational materials for the public, and current research and policy analysis concerning abortion and women's health issues. Copies of these materials and others are available for purchase and download on the organization's Web site.

National Organization for Women (NOW)
1100 H Street NW, 3rd Floor, Washington, DC   20005
(202) 628-8669 • fax: (202) 785-8576
Web site: www.now.org

The National Organization for Women (NOW) is a progressive feminist advocacy organization working to combat all forms of discrimination in the United States to ensure that women have the chance to fully participate in society and enjoy responsibilities and opportunities equal to men. The organization addresses issues such as abortion and reproductive rights, economic justice, and sex discrimination. NOW believes that safe and legal abortions should be available to all women without government restriction. Information about NOW's current campaigns, fact sheets, and other educational publications can be accessed online.

National Right to Life Committee (NRLC)

512 10th Street NW, Washington, DC 20004
(202) 626-8800
e-mail: NRLC@nrlc.org
Web site: www.nrlc.org

The National Right to Life Committee (NRLC) was formed in 1973 following the Supreme Court's decision in *Roe v. Wade*. The NRLC believes that human life should be protected from the time of conception and hopes to one day see the *Roe* decision overturned and a federal ban on abortion enacted. The organization advocates pro-life policies by lobbying Congress and providing information to the public about the horrors of abortion. NRLC's monthly publication, *National Right to Life News*, is available online.

Planned Parenthood Federation of America (PPFA)

434 West 33rd Street, New York, NY 10001
(212) 541-7800 • fax: (212) 245-1845
Web site: www.plannedparenthood.org

Planned Parenthood Federation of America (PPFA) provides reproductive health care to individuals in need, information about options for family planning, sex education, and aid to organizations with similar missions worldwide. The organization works through its local offices around the United States to offer women and men affordable services to prevent unintended pregnancy and sexually transmitted diseases. Planned Parenthood is an advocate of pro-choice policies and provides information on its Web site about the safety of abortion and the importance of continuing to keep abortion legal in the United States. In addition to information about abortion issues, the Web site contains information about birth control, emergency contraception, sexually transmitted diseases, global reproductive rights, and sex education programs that are not based on abstinence.

Population Connection

2120 L Street NW, Suite 500, Washington, DC   20037
(202) 332-2200 • fax: (202) 332-2302
e-mail: info@populationconnection.com
Web site: www.populationconnection.org

Population Connection, formerly Zero Population Growth, educates people about the dangers of the world's growing population and offers methods to stabilize the global population. The organization also focuses on women's reproductive health as a means to control population growth, promoting alternatives to abstinence-only sex education, and access to family planning programs and pro-choice policies worldwide. Population Control's official magazine, the *Reporter*, is published tri-annually. Electronic archives of this publication, reports, and fact sheets are available on the organization's Web site.

Priests for Life

PO Box 141172, Staten Island, NY   10314
(718) 980-4400 • fax: (718) 980-6515
e-mail: mail@priestsforlife.org
Web site: www.priestsforlife.org

Priests for Life was formed with the goal of vocally and actively opposing abortion and euthanasia worldwide. The organization promotes the belief that abortion is murder with the hopes that the practice will be banned. Priests for Life has founded programs such as Silent No More, which publicizes the effects of abortion on men, women, and their families. The organization also publicizes graphic images of aborted fetuses and abortion procedures to convince Americans that abortion should be banned. Additional information can be accessed on the organization's Web site.

United States Conference of Catholic Bishops (USCCB)

3211 Fourth Street NE, Washington, DC   20017
(202) 541-3000
Web site: www.usccb.org

United States Conference of Catholic Bishops (USCCB) seeks to advance the ministry of Catholic bishops through evangelization. Abortion and the promotion of pro-life policies worldwide exist at the center of the organization's advocacy efforts. The USCCB provides extensive information about abortion on their Web site, including church documents, teachings, articles, publications, testimony, and letters. Specific abortion-related issues addressed by the organization include the Freedom of Choice Act, partial-birth abortions, and international abortion issues.

Bibliography of Books

Books

Erika Bachiochi · *The Cost of "Choice": Women Evaluate the Impact of Abortion.* New York: Encounter, 2004.

Jennifer Baumgardner · *Abortion & Life.* New York: Akashic, 2008.

Francis J. Beckwith · *Defending Life: A Moral and Legal Case Against Abortion Choice.* New York: Cambridge University Press, 2007.

David Boonin · *A Defense of Abortion.* New York: Cambridge University Press, 2002.

Anne Hendershott · *The Politics of Abortion.* New York: Encounter, 2006.

N.E.H. Hull and Peter Charles Hoffer · *Roe v. Wade: The Abortion Rights Controversy in American History.* Lawrence: University Press of Kansas, 2001.

Krista Jacob, ed. · *Our Choices, Our Lives: Unapologetic Writings on Abortion.* Bloomington, IN: iUniverse, 2004.

Susan A. Martinelli-Fernandez, Lori Baker-Sperry, and Heather McIlvaine-Newsad, eds.	*Interdisciplinary Views on Abortion: Essays from Philosophical, Sociological, Anthropological, Political, Health and Other Perspectives.* Jefferson, NC: McFarland, 2009.
Eileen L. McDonagh	*Breaking the Abortion Deadlock: From Choice to Consent.* New York: Oxford University Press, 1996.
Kathleen McDonnell	*Not an Easy Choice: A Feminist Re-Examines Abortion.* Toronto, Ontario, Canada: Second Story, 2003.
Vasu Murti and Carol Crossed	*The Liberal Case Against Abortion.* Grand Rapids, MI: R.A.G.E. Media, 2006.
Bernard N. Nathanson	*The Hand of God: A Journey from Death to Life by the Abortion Doctor Who Changed His Mind.* Washington, DC: Regnery, 2001.
Marvin Olasky and William J. Bennett	*Abortion Rites: A Social History of Abortion in America.* Wheaton, IL: Crossway, 1992.
Rosalind P Petchesky	*Abortion and Woman's Choice: The State, Sexuality, and Reproductive Freedom.* Boston, MA: Northeastern University Press, 1985.
John Joseph Powell	*Abortion: The Silent Holocaust.* Allen, TX: Tabor, 1981.

Leslie J. Reagan	*When Abortion Was a Crime: Women, Medicine, and Law in the United States, 1867–1973.* Berkeley: University of California Press, 1998.
Daniel Schiff	*Abortion in Judaism.* New York: Cambridge University Press, 2002.
Rickie Solinger	*Abortion Wars: A Half Century of Struggle, 1950–2000.* Berkeley: University of California Press, 1998.
Michael Tooley et al.	*Abortion: Three Perspectives.* New York: Oxford University Press, 2009.
Laurence H. Tribe	*Abortion: The Clash of Absolutes.* New York: Norton, 1992.
Susan Wicklund and Alan S. Kesselheim	*This Common Secret: My Journey as an Abortion Doctor.* New York: Public Affairs, 2008.

Index

P

Parental consent laws
  abortion pill, 152
  are necessary, 76–81
  are unnecessary, 82–86
  emergency contraception, 132
Parental leave and family government support, 109
Parental notification laws, 76, 78–79, 80–81, 83
  See also Parental consent laws
Parenting
  sacrifices, 34, 37–38, 115
  single-parent families, 16, 126, 128
Partial-Birth Abortion Ban Act (2003), 67–68, 73–74, 172, 174
Partial-birth abortions. *See* Late-term abortions
People for the Ethical Treatment of Animals (PETA), 37
Personal bodily rights, 20–21
  late-term abortion and, 70
  make abortion morally just, 27, 32, 39
Personal decision making
  factors influencing, 17
  individualism vs. social consciousness, 92–94, 95–96
  moral capabilities of humans, 15, 20–21, 31
Personal responsibility, 95–96, 103, 108
Personhood
  legislation attempts, 57–58
  pro-choice views, 23, 31, 42, 63, 94, 112, 160
  pro-life views, 23–24, 46, 57–58, 63–64, 94–95
  See also Fetuses

Personhood of Children Act (HB 1572), North Dakota, 57
Pew Research Center surveys, 20, 97
Pharmacists, prescription refusals, 29
Philip, Diana, 82–86
Plan B, 29, 131–132
Planned Parenthood
  mental health problem denials, 160, 161–163, 167
  motto and advertising, 47
  press, 64
  socioeconomics of abortion, 90
Planned Parenthood of Southeastern Pennsylvania v. Casey (1992), 68
Political aspects, abortion debate
  abortion as wedge voting issue, 28, 65, 98
  campaign rhetoric, 77, 81
  elections, 28, 51, 65, 92
  late/partial birth abortion bans, 62, 64–65, 67–68, 73–74
  personhood and informed consent bills, 57–58
  political integrity, 96–99
  "political momentum," 17
  studies, abortion and women's health, 89–90, 168–169, 174, 176
Polls. *See* Public opinion
Posner, Richard, 61–62
Post-abortion emotional problems
  are rare, 171–178
  men, 166
  real harms to women, 159–170

Langston Hughes

by Jennifer Joline Anderson

Content Consultant
Christopher C. De Santis, Professor of African American
Literature, Illinois State University

CORE
LIBRARY

Published by ABDO Publishing Company, PO Box 398166, Minneapolis, MN 55439. Copyright © 2013 by Abdo Consulting Group, Inc. International copyrights reserved in all countries. No part of this book may be reproduced in any form without written permission from the publisher. The Core Library™ is a trademark and logo of ABDO Publishing Company.

Printed in the United States of America,
North Mankato, Minnesota
112012
012013

♻ THIS BOOK CONTAINS AT LEAST 10% RECYCLED MATERIALS.

Editor: Kari Cornell
Series Designer: Becky Daum

Cataloging-in-Publication Data
Anderson, Jennifer Joline.
  Langston Hughes / Jennifer Joline Anderson.
    p. cm. -- (Great American authors)
Includes bibliographical references and index.
ISBN 978-1-61783-718-0
1. Hughes, Langston, 1902-1967--Juvenile literature. 2. Poets, American--19th century--Biography--Juvenile literature. 3. African-American poets--19th century--Biography--Juvenile literature.   I. Title.
818/.5209--dc23
[B]   2012946815

Photo Credits: Hulton Archive/Getty Images, cover, 1; Fred Stein Archive/Getty Images, 4; Library of Congress, 7, 23, 45; Apic/Getty Images, 10; AP Images, 12, 34; North Wind/North Wind Picture Archives, 15; Red Line Editorial, 19, 39; Universal History Archive/Getty Images, 20; Olga Matseyko/Shutterstock Images, 25; Bettmann/Corbis/AP Images, 26, 29, 31, 37; Bebeto Matthews/AP Images, 41

CONTENTS

CHAPTER ONE

Becoming a Poet

Langston Hughes was on a train to Mexico in 1920 when he was 17 years old. It was a long trip from Cleveland, Ohio, to his father's ranch in the town of Toluca. Langston was feeling gloomy. His parents separated when Langston was small, and he had only seen his father a few times. They did not get along. Now he had just graduated from high

Langston Hughes sitting at his desk in 1954

school and would be spending the summer with his father. He was not sure how the trip would go.

When he was sad, Langston always poured his feelings into poetry. He got out his pen and an envelope he had in his pocket. The train was just crossing the Mississippi River, and Langston gazed down at the muddy waters below. He thought of his ancestors, the African-American people who had been sold into slavery. They had traveled down this same river to the plantations of the South. Then his mind wandered to other rivers in the world. He thought of the Congo in the heart of Africa and the Nile in Egypt. He thought of the Euphrates in Asia, where ancient civilizations had begun.

"I've known rivers," he wrote. "My soul has grown deep like the rivers." His hand moved quickly as he scribbled the lines on the back of the envelope. Fifteen minutes later, he had written a new poem, "The Negro Speaks of Rivers." Later that summer, he sent the poem to Jessie Fauset, a black editor and

Langston often turned to poetry to express his feelings. Many of his poems speak of his African-American pride.

writer in New York. She published the poem in *The Crisis*, an African-American magazine, when Langston was 19. It was the first time one of his poems appeared in a major publication. It was written in simple language yet had deep meaning.

Following a Dream

During that summer with his father, Langston wrote many poems. He felt out of place in his father's world. James Hughes was wealthy and successful. But he was also bitter and angry. He had moved to Mexico because laws in the United States made it impossible for him to practice law. Now he wanted Langston to leave America too. He wanted Langston to go to school in Switzerland and Germany, where he could learn to be an engineer. Then he could find a good job in Mexico working for a mining company.

Langston did not like this idea. Engineers needed to use a lot of math. Langston didn't want to study math, especially in a different language. He knew he wanted to be a writer, not an engineer. And he did not want to go to Switzerland or Germany. Instead, he had another place in mind: Harlem, New York.

To Langston Harlem was a dream city. It was a center of culture that attracted people of color from around the world. Many black musicians, actors, artists, and thinkers lived and worked in Harlem. He longed to see new black musicals on Broadway and hear the latest jazz and blues music in the nightclubs. He wanted to experience a city bustling with

Harlem, New York

Harlem is a neighborhood in Manhattan, which is part of New York City. In the early 1900s, large numbers of black people from the South moved to Harlem in search of a better life. Since then, the population of Central Harlem has been mostly African American. In the 1920s, Harlem was the center of an international black arts and culture movement known as the Harlem Renaissance. Langston Hughes was very involved in the movement. His stories and poems captured the spirit of Harlem.

Poet and playwright Langston Hughes in his 20s

people who were black like him. And he wanted to write about it all.

At last Langston's father agreed to send him to Columbia University in Harlem. Langston left for New York City in the fall of 1921. He never did study engineering. Instead he followed his own path.

"The Negro Speaks of Rivers"

I've known rivers:

I've known rivers ancient as the world and older than the

flow of human blood in human veins.

My soul has grown deep like the rivers.

I bathed in the Euphrates when dawns were young.

I built my hut near the Congo and it lulled me to sleep.

I looked upon the Nile and raised the pyramids above it.

I heard the singing of the Mississippi when Abe Lincoln

went down to New Orleans, and I've seen its muddy

bosom turn all golden in the sunset.

I've known rivers:

Ancient, dusky rivers.

My soul has grown deep like the rivers.

Source: Langston Hughes. "The Negro Speaks of Rivers," The Crisis,
June 1921. Print. 71.

What's the Big Idea?

Read this poem carefully. How do you think the poet is feeling? Is the voice he uses happy or sad? What is the poem's main idea?

CHAPTER TWO

Growing Up

James Langston Hughes was born in Joplin, Missouri, on February 1, 1902. He was named after his father, James Hughes, but his family called him Langston. His parents separated when he was a baby. He lived with his mother, Carrie Mercer Langston, but she struggled to support her only child. She moved to different cities to find jobs. She left Langston to be raised by his grandmother, Mary Leary

A young Langston Hughes in his boyhood hometown of Lawrence, Kansas, in 1914

Raid at Harpers Ferry

In October 1859 abolitionist John Brown and several others raided a military arms warehouse at Harpers Ferry, West Virginia. They planned to take all the weapons and start a rebellion against slavery. Their plan failed. All the men were either captured or killed, and John Brown was hanged. But the daring raid at Harpers Ferry lit a spark. Two years and many more clashes later, the Civil War began. By the end of the war, slavery was outlawed in the United States.

Langston, in Lawrence, Kansas.

Grandma Mary's Stories

Grandma Mary was a gentle, dignified woman. Langston loved her very much, but he was lonely without his parents or any siblings. They were poor and often had only salt pork and wild dandelion greens to eat. When Langston felt sad and alone, he escaped into the wonderful world of stories. His grandmother had many magazines and books in the house, and he read them all. But he especially loved to sit on his

Abolitionist John Brown holds one of his dying sons in the Battle of Harpers Ferry.

grandmother's lap while she told him about heroes from the past.

The stories she told were all true. Grandma Mary's first husband, Lewis Sheridan Leary, had died in the famous slave revolt at Harpers Ferry, West Virginia. His grandfather, Charles Langston, was an abolitionist who spoke out against slavery. His great-uncle, John Mercer Langston, had been the first black Congressman from the state of Virginia. Her stories made Langston proud to be an African American. Years later, he wrote a poem called "Aunt Sue's Stories," inspired by his Grandma Mary.

Langston's grandmother died when he was 12 years old. Remembering her stories made him brave. "Nobody ever cried in my grandmother's stories. They worked, or schemed, or fought. But no crying. When my grandmother died, I didn't cry, either," Langston later wrote in his autobiography.

Class Poet

After Grandma Mary died, Langston moved to Lincoln, Illinois, to live with his mother. Langston started eighth grade at a new school. He and one other girl were the only black students. He was popular and known as a good writer. Langston was elected class poet. At graduation he read a poem he had written about his teachers and classmates.

In 1916 the family moved to Cleveland, Ohio, and Langston went to Central High School. There he had friends who were black and white, Jewish and

Catholic. He published poems in the school magazine, *The Belfry Owl*.

Cleveland and the Great Migration

When Langston and his family lived in Cleveland, the city had a large population of African Americans. Most of them came from the South. They had moved north during the Great Migration to escape racism in the southern states. But racial discrimination was strong in the north as well. Black people were only welcome in certain neighborhoods. Landlords charged black families higher rent than what white people paid.

Early Influences

One of Langston's favorite poets was Paul Laurence Dunbar (1872-1906). The son of former slaves, Dunbar became the first African-American poet to become known around the world. His poems often used African-American dialect, or the language of everyday conversation. Hughes found Dunbar's poetry real and inspiring. As a high school student, Langston wrote: "My soul is full of color / Like de wings of a butterfly." He was writing in the style of Dunbar.

Langston's family could only afford small, cramped attic or basement apartments.

African Americans also had more trouble finding work. His stepfather worked long, grueling hours at a steel mill. It made Langston sad to see his stepfather wearing himself away so the family could eat. Langston wrote a poem, "Steel Mills," in which he described the mills "That grind out steel / And grind away the lives / Of men."

Journey to Mexico

When Langston was 17 he spent the summer in Mexico with his father. He was not happy there. His father was rich. He owned a vast ranch and many apartment buildings in the city, but he treated his employees poorly. He even forced Langston to sit for hours adding up figures. "Seventeen and you can't add yet!" he would yell when the numbers did not add up right.

By the end of the summer Langston never wanted to see his father again. But after he graduated from

The Great Migration, 1910–1930		
City	African-American Population	
	1910	1930
Chicago, IL	44,103	134,000
Cleveland, OH	8,500	72,000
Detroit, MI	5,741	120,066
New York, NY	91,709	328,000
Philadelphia, PA	84,500	220,600
St. Louis, MO	45,000	94,000

The Great Migration

From 1910 to 1930, between 1.5 and 2 million blacks moved north to escape racism in the South. In just a few decades, large northern cities, including Cleveland and New York's Harlem neighborhood, became centers of African-American life. The Great Migration changed American culture in many ways. Look at the chart above. What does it tell you about the Great Migration?

high school, he returned to Mexico. He hoped to convince his father to send him to college. Langston showed his father his poem "The Negro Speaks of Rivers." It was printed in a magazine, *The Crisis*. Finally James Hughes gave in. If his son could get a poem published at such a young age, perhaps he could become a success after all.

CHAPTER THREE

Across the Ocean

Hughes enrolled at Columbia University in September of 1921, but he felt out of place in the mostly white school. After one year Hughes dropped out, and his father stopped sending him money. He looked for a job, but time and again he was told, "I didn't advertise for a colored boy." Finally, in June 1923, he was hired to work on a trade ship bound for Africa.

As a young man, Langston Hughes was drawn to the social scene in Harlem.

As the ship headed across the ocean, Hughes felt relieved and excited. He was 21 years old now, a grown man. And he was ready to learn from life.

African Shores

Hughes's ship stopped at ports in Senegal and Nigeria, on the western coast of Africa. Even here Africans were ruled by white people from Europe. The white people treated Africans unfairly, just as whites in America treated blacks unfairly. This made Hughes angry. He told the Africans he understood their problems because he was black too. To his shock, they didn't believe him—they thought he was a white man.

Like many African Americans, Hughes had a mixed racial background. His skin was coppery-

Inspired by Africa

Hughes was one of the first American poets to use African themes, or ideas, in his work. In Africa, he often heard the beat of African drums. One of his poems, "Danse Africaine," describes a dancer moving to the beat: "The low beating of the tom-toms . . . / Stirs your blood. / Dance!"

Langston Hughes poses for this photo by Gordon Parks in 1943.

brown, not black, and his hair was wavy, not curly. But he still felt a strong connection to the African people. He wrote many poems about his experiences on African shores and sent them home to Harlem. A whole page of Hughes's poems appeared in the August 1923 issue of *The Crisis*.

Springtime in Paris

In the spring of 1924 Hughes traveled to Paris with only seven dollars in his pocket. He struggled to find a job and a place to live. Fortunately, he found work in a nightclub. As he washed pots and pans in the kitchen, he heard the sounds of jazz and blues. African-American music was in style throughout Europe. Hughes included this beat and flavor in his poetry. One of his poems, "Negro Dancers," captured the rhythm of two people dancing to jazz. Hughes sent his poems home to New York, where they were published in three magazines.

Love in Paris

While in Paris Hughes fell in love with a girl named Anne. Her father was African and her mother was English. They talked of marriage, but Hughes felt he was too poor to support a wife and family. Anne's father also did not approve of the match, so the two parted ways. Hughes never married. He wrote a sad poem about his lost love called "The Breath of a Rose." In 1928, the poem was made into a song by the composer William Grant Still.

Paris felt like home to Langston. He loved hearing the rhythms of the African-American jazz and blues that were popular in the nightclubs there at the time.

FURTHER EVIDENCE

There is quite a bit of information about Hughes's travels in Chapter Three. How did his travels influence his writing? Read about Langston Hughes and find some of his poems on a Web site, or look in his autobiography *The Big Sea* to find more information about his travels around the world. Find a quote to support the idea that Hughes's travels inspired his writing. Does the quote you found add a new idea to the chapter?

Langston Hughes's Poetry
www.english.illinois.edu/maps/poets/g_l/hughes/hughes.htm

CHAPTER FOUR

Renaissance in Harlem

When Hughes returned from Europe he found his reputation as a poet had grown while he was away. Many people had read his poems in New York magazines, and they were anxious to meet him. But being a promising young poet did not bring a regular paycheck. Hughes lived with his mother and brother in Washington DC. He found work at a wet wash laundry. Later he worked

African Americans dance at a Harlem nightclub in the 1930s. Nightclubs were gathering spots for poets, artists, and musicians during the Harlem Renaissance.

as a busboy in a hotel restaurant, setting and clearing tables. The jobs were not glamorous or literary, but Hughes enjoyed spending time with ordinary working people. He wrote poems about the people he met. One of these poems, "A Song to a Negro Wash-Woman," was published in *The Crisis* in January 1925.

Hughes and the Renaissance

In the spring of 1925 Hughes received an award of $40 for a poem called "The Weary Blues." Later he included it in a brand-new book of poems, also called *The Weary Blues*. It was published in January 1926 by Knopf when

---

Busboy Poet

In December of 1925, the well-known poet Vachel Lindsay held a poetry reading at the hotel where Hughes worked. Hughes wanted to meet Lindsay and hear his poems. But black people were not allowed in the auditorium. So he copied three of his poems and set them beside Lindsay's dinner plate. The next day, Hughes learned Lindsay had read the poems to his audience. Newspapers carried the story that Vachel Lindsay had discovered a "busboy poet."

This famous photograph of the "busboy poet" was snapped by a press photographer after Langston's poetry was praised by well-known poet Vachel Lindsay.

29

Jazz and Blues

Jazz and blues are musical styles with African roots. Both were developed by African-American musicians between the late 1800s and the early 1900s. Blues came from African-American spirituals, or religious songs, as well as from work songs and chants sung by slaves as they worked. Jazz combines African rhythms with European musical styles. Hughes loved jazz and blues, and he often invited musicians to play along with him as he read his poetry.

Hughes was 24 years old. Critics loved the book.

In 1926 Hughes enrolled at Lincoln University, a black college in Pennsylvania. Every summer he went back to Harlem. This was the period known as the Harlem Renaissance. During the 1920s, the African-American art, literature, music, dance, and theater happening in Harlem became known around the world. For the first time African-American artists were being recognized. At the time blacks were often stereotyped as humble servants, clownlike characters, or evil thugs. But the black

African Americans dance the famous Jitterbug in a Harlem nightclub in the 1930s.

EXPLORE ONLINE

Langston Hughes was a key figure in the Harlem Renaissance. Read over the information on the Harlem Renaissance at the end of Chapter Four. Then visit the Web sites below to learn more. Compare and contrast the information in this book with the information you find online. What can you learn about Langston Hughes and the Harlem Renaissance from the Web sites?

The Harlem Renaissance
www.pbskids.org/bigapplehistory/arts/topic9.html
www.brainpop.com/socialstudies/ushistory/harlemrenaissance

people who appeared in the art and literature of the Harlem Renaissance were real and complex. Hughes's writing was at the center of the exciting new movement. His poetry spoke truthfully about the African-American experience—both the good and the bad. It had the rhythms of blues and jazz. And it was written in a simple, honest style that most people could understand and appreciate. It was no wonder Langston Hughes became known throughout the world as the voice of Harlem. He expressed the hopes and dreams of African-American people.

Excerpt from "My People"

Dream-singers,
Story-tellers,
Dancers,
Loud laughers in the hands of Fate—
    My people.
Dish-washers,
Elevator-boys,
Ladies' maids,
Crap-shooters,
Cooks,
Waiters,
Jazzers,
Nurses of babies,
Loaders of ships,
Porters,
Hairdressers,
Comedians in vaudeville
And band-men in circuses—
Dream-singers all,
Story-tellers all.
. . .

Source: Langston Hughes. "My People," The Crisis, June 1922. Print. 72.

Nice View

Hughes wanted African Americans to be recognized as equal to whites. What is he saying about African Americans in this poem? Compare this poem with "The Negro Speaks of Rivers" on page 11. How are they similar or different?

CHAPTER FIVE

Spreading the Message

After Hughes graduated from college in 1929, the Great Depression hit. Thousands of Americans were out of work, and nobody had money to spare for a book of poetry. So Hughes traveled around the country reading his poems. He charged whatever his hosts could afford—sometimes $50 or $25—and sometimes nothing at all.

This photo was taken in 1961, when Langston Hughes was active in the Civil Rights Movement.

Jim Crow Laws

Beginning in 1876 many states in the South passed laws that segregated blacks from whites. These laws were named Jim Crow laws. The laws stated that blacks could not attend school or eat in restaurants with whites. On public buses, they had to ride in the back. Some states passed laws that made it hard for blacks to vote. Black people who broke the laws were sometimes beaten or even killed.

In the South, Jim Crow laws made it difficult for Hughes to travel. Hotels and restaurants had signs saying, "No Negroes Allowed!" But he was welcomed in black colleges, clubs, and private homes.

Hearing Hughes speak opened the eyes of young African Americans. Some of his poems, such as "My People," praised the beauty of African Americans and encouraged black pride. Other poems used strong language to protest racism. This made southern whites angry. Hughes was banned from speaking in some places, and guards were hired to make sure violence didn't break out.

When Langston Hughes traveled during his poetry tour in the 1930s, he saw signs like this all over the southern United States.

Hughes ended his poetry tour in San Francisco, California. He had traveled across the country reading his poetry. In doing so, he spread an important message about racial equality.

More than a Poet

Hughes also wrote novels, short stories, a two-volume autobiography, and nonfiction books to teach young people about African-American heroes. He wrote operas, musicals, plays, and he even created his own theater company in Harlem in 1938. It was

Hughes on Broadway

Beginning in 1942, Hughes wrote a weekly column for a black newspaper called the *Chicago Defender*. The column featured a comical character named Jesse B. Semple, or "Simple." Through Simple, Hughes used humor to talk about serious racial issues. The character Simple became so popular that Hughes published five books and wrote a Broadway play based on his stories.

called the Harlem Suitcase Theater because all the equipment they had could fit into one suitcase.

Poetry and the Civil Rights Movement

Slavery had been outlawed in 1863, but the dream of racial equality kept getting put off. People grew tired of waiting. In the 1950s and 1960s, African-American anger fueled the Civil Rights Movement. During this time of social unrest, masses of people fought for African-American rights. Hughes expressed his anger in his poetry. He protested racism and called for America to fulfill the dream of equality for all citizens, white and black.

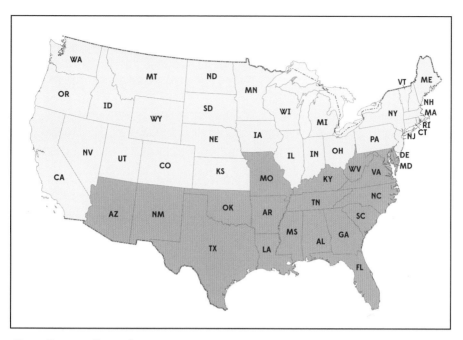

Jim Crow South

This map shows all the states that had Jim Crow laws in red. The laws were different from state to state. They separated blacks from whites in education, public transportation, hotels, restaurants, hospitals, prisons, and other areas of life. During the Civil Rights Movement, large groups of black people protested these racist laws.

Hughes dedicated his last book of poems, *The Panther and the Lash,* to Rosa Parks, a hero of the Civil Rights Movement.

A Writer's Legacy

Sadly, Hughes did not live to see the end of the Civil Rights Movement. He died suddenly after complications from surgery on May 22, 1967. Hughes's death was mourned all over the world. But his funeral was like a celebration. Jazz and blues music were played, and people read his poems aloud. His life's work had touched many people. Although people were sad when he died, they were grateful for the gifts he left behind.

During his lifetime, Hughes's writings spread the message of equality. His poems showed that black people were beautiful and had much to be proud of. They taught people of all races how to love themselves and each other. His success broke new ground for black writers everywhere. Today nearly 100 years after the Harlem Renaissance began, Hughes's works are still read and enjoyed. His influence remains strong and his legacy lives on.

The Langston Hughes House in Harlem, New York, is where the famous poet lived until his death in 1967. The house is now a historic landmark.

IMPORTANT DATES

1902
Hughes is born in Joplin, Missouri, on February 1.

1916
Moves with family to Cleveland, Ohio.

1920
Graduates from high school. Moves to Mexico to live with his father for the summer.

1921
His first national publication of a poem, "The Negro Speaks of Rivers," appears in *The Crisis* magazine. Moves to New York City to attend Columbia University.

1925
Discovered by poet Vachel Lindsay in December while working as a busboy in Washington DC.

1926
Enrolls at Lincoln University in January. His first book of poetry, *The Weary Blues,* is published.

1967
Dies in New York City on May 22 at the age of 65.

KEY WORKS

The Big Sea and *I Wonder As I Wander*

Hughes's two autobiographies. *The Big Sea* covers his early life and experiences during the Harlem Renaissance. *I Wonder As I Wander* covers the decades that follow.

Hughes, Langston. *The Big Sea*. New York: Knopf, 1940.

Hughes, Langston. *I Wonder As I Wander*. New York: Rinehart, 1956.

Five Plays

This collection of Hughes's plays includes *Mulatto*, his first Broadway play, and *Simply Heavenly*, a musical comedy based on the Simple character from Hughes's newspaper column.

Hughes, Langston. *Five Plays*. Ed. and Introd. Webster Smalley. Bloomington, IN: Indiana UP, 1963.

Montage of a Dream Deferred

This book contains a series of poems written in a jazz style. They show short scenes of life in Harlem and call out the need for social change and justice for African Americans.

Hughes, Langston. *Montage of a Dream Deferred*. New York: Holt, 1951.

Not Without Laughter

This novel tells about an African-American boy named Sandy. Hughes based the book partly on his own memories of growing up in Lawrence, Kansas.

Hughes, Langston. *Not Without Laughter*. New York: Knopf, 1930.

The Weary Blues

Hughes's first poetry collection, this book contains some of his most famous works, including the title poem "The Weary Blues," "The Negro Speaks of Rivers," and "Aunt Sue's Stories."

Hughes, Langston. *The Weary Blues*. New York: Knopf, 1926.

Take a Stand

This book discusses how Hughes tried to use his poems to spread a message about racism. Do you think poetry can really make a difference in the world? Write a short essay detailing your opinion, reasons for your opinion, and facts and details that support those reasons.

Dig Deeper

What questions do you still have about Langston Hughes? Do you want to learn more about his life or read some of his poems, stories, and plays for yourself? Write down one or two questions to help guide you in your research. With an adult's help, find reliable new sources about Langston's life and work that can help answer your questions. Write a few sentences about how you did your research and what you learned from it.

You Are There

Imagine that you visited Harlem during the 1920s, at the height of the Harlem Renaissance. Write 300 words describing your stay. What bands or musical acts did you see? Which authors and artists did you meet?

Tell the Tale

This book discusses Langston Hughes's life. Write 200 words that summarize the true story of how he became a writer. Be sure to set the scene, develop a sequence of events, and write a conclusion.

GLOSSARY

abolitionist
a person fighting to abolish, or end, slavery

autobiography
a story of a person's life, written by that person

civil rights
rights held by a citizen of a free nation

discrimination
unfair treatment of a group of people based on race, gender, age, religion, or some other characteristic

Great Migration
the mass movement of southern African Americans to the North to escape racism during the early 20th century

heritage
something that is passed down or inherited

legacy
something passed down from one generation to the next

novel
a long work of fiction

protest
to stand up against an idea or law

racism
unfair treatment of people based on their race

segregated
separated by race

stereotype
an overly simple opinion about a person or group

LEARN MORE

Books

Hughes, Langston. *Langston Hughes.* Ed. David Roessel and Arnold Rampersad. Illus. Benny Andrews. New York: Sterling Publishing, 2006.

Hughes, Langston. *The Big Sea: An Autobiography.* 1940. New York: Hill and Wang, 1993.

Walker, Alice. *Langston Hughes: American Poet.* Illus. Catherine Deeter. New York: HarperCollins, 1974, 2002.

Web Links

To learn more about Langston Hughes, visit ABDO Publishing Company online at **www.abdopublishing.com.** Web sites about Langston Hughes are featured on our Book Links page. These links are routinely monitored and updated to provide the most current information available.
Visit **www.mycorelibrary.com** for free additional tools for teachers and students.

INDEX

ABOUT THE AUTHOR

Jennifer Joline Anderson has been writing since she was a teenager. She lives with her husband and children, Alex, Ruby, and Henry, in Minneapolis, Minnesota, where she writes educational books for young people.